INDIA

A FEW PAGES ABOUT IT

INDIA

A FEW PAGES ABOUT IT

SIR EDWARD WILLIAM WATKIN

GYAN

Published by

Gyan Publishing House
5, Ansari Road
Daryaganj, New Delhi-110002
Phone: 011-47034999, 9811692060
E-mail: books@gyanbooks.com

Distribution Network
gyanbooks.com
India, USA, Canada, UK, Australia

ISBN: 978-93-7014-976-2 (PB)

First Published, 1889

2nd Impression 2025

Printed at: Gyan Press, Delhi.

INDIA A FEW PAGES ABOUT IT

Arthur SIR EDWARD WILLIAM WATKIN

India.

India:

A FEW PAGES ABOUT IT.

BY

SIR EDWARD WILLIAM WATKIN, BART., M.P.

1889.

London:
C. F. ROWORTH, GREAT NEW STREET, FETTER LANE.
—
1889

These few pages are offered to the MOST HONORABLE THE

MARQUIS OF SALISBURY, K.G.,

HER MAJESTY'S PRIME MINISTER,

Formerly Secretary of State for India,

—in the hope that the vast resources of India may be fully, and soon, developed; that Indian Railways may be extended and commercialised; and that a paternal Government may spare no efforts towards strengthening the competitive powers of the cultivator and merchant of a wonderful country; so that Protection in America may be met by Production in India.

E. W. W.

NORTHENDEN,
June, 1889.

CONTENTS.

INTRODUCTORY AND PERSONAL.

ON the eve of my leaving England for India in October last a high official was good enough to invite me to suggest to him any notions which, in travelling about, might strike me—especially in reference to railway and industrial development. I complied with his wish from time to time; and on my return I sent to him some time ago a copy of some notes I made on the voyage home.

I now somewhat expand those notes for the use, primarily, of a few friends, and relatives, of my own.

Having been a student of India, and in communication with people of all sorts interested in India, all my life, my visit to the country has pieced together the links of previous knowledge and given me some better insight into questions, many of which it would require almost a lifetime to master. But I am not immodest enough to consider that much that I may in all good faith propose, is not capable of modification by larger experiences, if not of much correction. Therefore it is that in these pages I have confined myself, mainly, to matters which I understand, and I doubt if, therefore, I can be much mistaken, save as respects the adaptation of Indian agencies to western practice. The leaders in all industrial progress in India, as it seems to me, have been, are, and must be, as a rule, men of

British and European race. The white man rules in India, industrially, by reason not merely of his courage and force of character, but through the completeness of his experience.

What can be a better illustration than the tea planting? a new and modern industry in India. Three hundred thousand acres of Indian land are planted with tea, of which two hundred thousand are in Assam. If the total were divided by the average size of the plantations, there would turn out to be probably about one thousand separate organizations for the growth and sale of tea; and I doubt not that almost the whole are ruled over by British people, and have been founded and worked by the agency of British capital.*

The European merchant and government of India have between them developed the supply of jute and cotton, and so with everything else.

British capital has made almost all the railways, docks, and other public works of India; and British men must and will lead where, in time, the Mussulman and the Hindoo may follow. In writing this I am not indifferent to the enterprise of the Parsees, the Jews of India, as they are called, or to the extraordinary push of the smaller native merchant, who follows a traveller about and noses out a possible customer wherever he may be—in bed, shaving, bathing, walking out, or sitting in his room; or to the patient industry of the people who do the hand labour and art labour of the country.

Succinctly, the suggestions I humbly venture to make as the result of my observation and enquiry are:—(1) The establishment of a powerful department of the Indian State, consisting of

---

* In passing, I may remind those who read these pages, that Ceylon is becoming a great tea-growing country, thanks, mainly, to the initiative of my friend, Mr. George Wall, of Colombo, and to the persistent efforts and thorough enterprise of English planters like Mr. Thring, and others. Tea, in Ceylon, is making up for the loss of the coffee crop. In past times the export of coffee from Ceylon was valued at about seven millions sterling a year; now, the fatal fungus, which has so widely ruined the crop, has brought the production down to a little more than a tenth of its old average value. And a comparatively small number of years ago, all the Cingalese consumption of tea was derived from China, and a little later from China and India.

practical men, which, provided with adequate means and with the fullest powers, shall develop thoroughly the undeveloped mineral and other resources of India, especially its coal and petroleum. (2) The extension of Indian railways and works, by the economical credit and efficient organization of the Indian State. (3) The commercialisation of the Indian Railway system, giving business, rather than military, management. (4) A complete change in the storage and warehousing system. (5) The laying down of independent submarine cables by the State, and the provision of far cheaper means of passing to and fro between the United Kingdom and India.

I shall endeavour to show by what the Indian State organization now does, that it can do more, and that the Indian civil servant—if given full responsibility and if freed from needless interference, either from Downing Street, Calcutta, or Simla—is fully equal to any task placed on his shoulders in the interests of India. Let me, however, say that the military servant is, to my mind, an excellent public officer; that where he has been allowed to construct and work, for instance, the railway system, in his own way, he has been equal to any, and every, difficult occasion. But the trouble comes from head-quarters, in the constant attempt to apply military rule to industrial distribution, and in delays and cross purposes by too much reference home of details.

But I shall endeavour to show, further, by the many failures of most efforts to substitute "private enterprise" for the action of the State, that the great, immediate, wide-spread development of the undeveloped riches of India can only be thoroughly accomplished, in our time, by the united and unsparing efforts of the Indian State itself.

"VISIT INDIA!"

I had all my life a desire to visit India. I once, a very long time ago, was nearly precipitated into an Indian career. I had taken much interest in the Indian railway system; in the affairs of Ceylon; in the growth of cotton in India, and so on, for very many years.*

---

* As an amusing incident, I may relate that, in early childhood, I narrowly escaped sudden death owing, remotely, to the modification of the Indian tea monopoly. The facts were these: the date was about 1826 or 1828; the close monopoly of the sale of tea had led to "gunpowder" tea being considered cheap at a guinea a pound; gunpowder and guinea made a good practical alliteration; in trade, one was the equivalent of the other. The relaxation of the monopoly—I quite forget the form and extent of relaxation—enabled enterprising tea dealers largely to reduce prices, and the result was, that an enterprising firm—"Jones & Co.," tea dealers, Market Street Lane, Manchester—advertised that, incredible as it might appear, they would be prepared to sell "gunpowder tea" for "ten shillings and sixpence a pound." I must now remind, or rather inform, the reader—assumed to have been born since the enlightened period in question—that the ladies of the house regarded tea in those days as a precious, almost a sacred, article. The "tea-caddy" was a sort of jewel-box. It had always a key. It was always kept locked for fear some Tabitha might be tempted to abstract a spoonful of the valued thing; and a lady going out to dinner, or even to a ball, would often turn pale and stop the coach, with the ejaculation to her astonished husband, "Oh, dear! I have left behind the key of the tea-caddy!" Tea, thus, *was* tea in those days. In those days ladies wore "gigot" sleeves and high "waists," in compliment to the Queen, whose natural shape was, they said, the same from the hips to the armpits. Whether it was so I am unable to say; I am only positive on the fact of the ladies' dresses. But the effect of these fashions led to much display of redundant bombazine, as the fashionable material then in vogue was called. My escape from sudden death arose thus:—I was taken "a-shopping" by my mother, who had an eye to business, and quite understood that a guinea would, now, go as far as two would have gone before. So we entered the shop of "Jones & Co.," of Market Street Lane, Manchester, with a crowd of housewives, who, by their struggles to the counters, made "confusion worse confounded," and my poor little child-body was soon lost amidst the bombazine. I was crushed, smothered, warmed up to a high degree, and imbibed an odour of bombazine, &c., &c., which I can (as the Scotch put it as to smells) "feel" to this day! How I got out I know not. In the dark and dismal surroundings—hot smelling, suffocating—I fancy I lost consciousness; fancied I was drowning; and striking out in the darkness frantically, did some injury to a very fat woman, who thereon backed lesser women out, and I was restored to air and daylight.

But at that time no tea was brought from India: it all came from China, and the East India Company had a close monopoly. Their old tea warehouses in Mint Street in the City are now the property of the London and North Western Railway Company. After my little story of suffering and miraculous escape, none of my friends will wonder at the great interest I have always taken in the tea question. Any way, I have suggested a way to more than

I need not recall the sorrow which compelled me, in search of forgetfulness, to go a long way from home somewhere. I had been thirty times across the Atlantic, the last voyage having been in 1887, and I therefore gravitated to India as a new field.

My visit gave me incredible interest: and to all who want to see the real British Empire, I cannot hesitate to recommend my own example: I say, emphatically, "Visit India!" To all who want to observe how the moral force of a small body of our countrymen prevails in keeping the peace amidst the most hostile creeds and races; to watch the processes by which a most just, impartial, and capable government is furnished to over 200,000,000 of people—who never knew real liberty, either civil or religious, until they obtained the blessing—the priceless blessing—of British paternal rule—to all these I say, "Visit India." To all who want to see grand rivers, stately mountains, and wondrous plains, I say again, "Visit India." It is a land of wonders all round.

To the naturalist, the geologist, the scientist of every division, India is an infinite field of observation. There, too, you see, side by side, in many places, almost every race of man the world contains.

I shall never forget the sight at Darjeeling: Chinese, Burmese, Tibetans, Nepaulese, Bhotans, Nagas, Hindoos, Mussulmen; men the exact pattern of the red Indian of the Canadian Pacific route, and of the yellow Indian of British Columbia; English types, German types—every type almost.

Every variety of man. Every species of animal, plant, flower, reptile. Every variety of custom, and of social life.

Architecture of the most opposite ideality, but often massive and magnificent; dress as varied as race.

Agriculture so different from ours; but when studied found

---

one Chancellor of the Exchequer, by which the duty on tea could be repealed without putting on any new tax. But my plan is too simple for official acceptance. I certainly hope that every poor soul who has now to pay 2*s*. 6*d*. for a pound of what, at prime cost, grown in India, and delivered in England, only stands at 6¾*d*., will soon be able to have three cups of tea for what is now the price of one.

to be simple, and therefore scientific—the most being made of the simplest and readiest means.

MY ROUTE IN INDIA.

I left the Thames in the P. and O. ship, the "Arcadia," commanded by that veteran sailor, Captain Andrews. I landed at Gibraltar, Marseilles, Naples, and Port Said. The ship stopped at Aden, and arrived at Bombay after a voyage without a breeze or a drop of rain. At Bombay the kindness of Messrs. Ralli, the great merchants of India, enabled me to see something of the industries and the commerce of that remarkable city. From Bombay, following the good advice of Sir Michael Biddulph, I went right away north and up the Khyber Pass till within view of Allah Musjid, stopping on the way at Ajmere, Jeypore, Delhi, Lahore, and Peshawur. Returning, I visited Rawul Pindi, Lahore again, the salt ranges at Kewrah, Umritser, Agra, Cawnpore, Lucknow, Allahabad, and other centres, and then went down to Calcutta, where I had the happiness to be the guest of Mr. Henry Gladstone, in Clive Street. Then, after some days at this great port, I went by way of the Eastern Bengal Railway up to Darjeeling, in sight of the vast Himalayas, and back to Siligouri, from whence across country and across rivers to Dhubri, thence up the Brahmapootra to Dibrughar, and on to the farthest corner of Assam up to the Naga country, the limit of British territory to the north-east. Then returning to Calcutta, I had the diversion of a slight earthquake, and after a Christmas dinner at Mr. Gladstone's, I left for Colombo in the "Rohilla," Captain Haslewood. Spent two days in Ceylon, going up to Kandy, and then on to Aden, Suez, Port Said, Marseilles, and home.

Murray's Guide or Baedeker give better descriptions of places of interest and of scenery than I could, so I do not propose to attempt anything of that sort. But for all things archæological, I refer every one to General Cunningham's excellent and interesting works on the monumental and other remains of India.

FACTS ABOUT INDIA.

It is well to tabulate some leading facts about British India, and I have done so in a final chapter. Two Parliamentary Blue Books are annually issued. I shall have a few words to write about the backward dates of much of the information given; but they will throw no doubt upon the great value of the insight afforded. They are the "Statement exhibiting the moral and material progress and condition of India," and the "Statistical Abstract relating to British India," which gives a decennial tabulation, and may compare with that afforded by the similar "Statistical Abstract" more especially affecting the United Kingdom. If some one would, to use a phrase of the late Mr. W. Newmarch, F.R.S., "boil down" these papers, and let them be sold for a few pence, a great national service would be performed. Our people would read India by the light of its progress, instead of seeing it in the disguises exhibited now and then by the Indian, or Russian, agents of discontent, some of whom live amongst us in apparent personal prosperity. These gentlemen would have us to believe that the Indian Government is an unenlightened tyrant, that the population of the country is on the wane, its wealth decreasing and misery augmenting. All this is untrue: nay, the very converse of the truth, as the facts and figures quoted in my concluding chapter demonstrate.

INDIAN RAILWAYS AND INDIAN SUPPLIES.

I AM somewhat informed about Indian Railways and their history. As early as the 17th July, 1857, I moved this Resolution in the House of Commons:—"That the slow progress of the East Indian Railways involves danger to the military occupation of India, and retards the development of the industrial resources of that country"; and I concluded my speech with these words: —"India had, physically speaking, all that was necessary for a rapid and full development, except the means of transit. Cease to keep from her those means, and she would, in spite of mismanagement, and of internal disorders, rise in the industrial scale; and the very measures which promoted her prosperity would consolidate our power." I see nothing to correct in that declaration of nearly a generation ago.

My personal observations of Indian Railways have greatly impressed me with admiration for those who have planned and executed, and especially for those who now work, them, under conditions of difficulty unknown at home. I do not think that I write, biassed by the extreme courtesy shown to me by every railway man I knew, and by numbers of others whose acquaintance I made for the first time. These gentlemen aided me in every way to conquer the vast distances of India, and, by travelling at night in their comfortable officers' carriages, through wastes and jungles, as well as cultivated lands, to visit the places and scenes of great interest, otherwise shut to me in a visit of under two months. To Colonel Campbell, the honoured agent of the East Indian; Major Bissett, of the Bombay and Baroda; Colonel Wallace, of the North Western State, and Major Boughey, of the Eastern Bengal State,—Railways, I am specially debtor, for every form of kindness and facility to inspect the magnificent undertakings, happily, under their control.

Having thus travelled over more than a third of the whole mileage of Indian railways, I return with unmixed respect for the works and the workers. I have travelled on the Government gauge of 5 ft. 6 in.; the "metre" gauge of thirty-nine inches; the 2 ft. 6 in. gauge; and the 1 ft. 11 in. gauge of the wonderful Darjeeling railway. Nowhere have I seen works more daring—often to the point of grandeur—and I have, specially, in my mind, while writing, the bridge over the Indus, below its junction with the Cabul river, at Attock; Sir Bradford Leslie's bridge over the Hooghly, above Calcutta (the Jubilee Bridge); and, I might add, the Great Indian Peninsular Station at Bombay—these are many and varied Indian monuments of the art of our engineers and contractors, working in India in wider fields than home presents. I was disappointed in finding myself unable, owing to time used in visiting Assam, to see the Sukkur Bridge over the Indus, or to go up to Quetta—where I was most kindly invited by Sir R. Sandeman—to see the new (Sind Pishin) railways there, and the petroleum springs near Sibi.

The story of the construction of these Quetta railway works reads like a romance, and excites admiration for the courage and resources of the engineers, proving them to be men who would not be beaten.

The report on Indian Railways for 1886 says, "From the 8th May, 1886, and onwards, from mile 175 the plate-laying was pushed forward uninterruptedly, and with no very heavy diversions, Harnai being reached on the 1st July, 1886, and mile 201 on the 1st August, 1886. The heat throughout this whole time was terrific, and so trying, that, on many occasions, it seemed impossible to go on with the work. The staff suffered terribly from fever; the plate-laying gangs were practically renewed every month by fresh importations from India, as they melted away from fever, dysentery and scurvy. In the same way, the gangs of girder-erectors dropped off, and during four months were twice replaced from India. . . . . On the 1st November, 1886, the rail-head had reached mile 224 (opposite the mouth of the Chupper Rift), passing over many diversions, where heavy girders were being erected and difficult foundations of bridges were being taken out. Although the higher elevation reached somewhat reduced the heat, the exceptional unhealthiness of the climate retarded the work, whole gangs of workmen being prostrated at one time by fever, dysentery and scurvy." I will only give one more extract, and then say, "All honour to our countrymen, who can trample on such difficulties!" "The line viâ Harnai, from Sibi to Quetta (155 miles), was practically commenced as a railway only about 1st July, 1884. It labours under the disadvantage of its lower half being so hot in summer, and its upper half so cold in winter, that on those sections, as far as progress is concerned, about half the year is lost. This section was opened for the engine as a permanently bridged, metalled and tunnelled railway in 32½ months, giving a progress of little less than five miles of finished railway per month, in a mountainous country, where the engineering difficulties, though formidable enough in themselves, are not, perhaps, the greatest obstacle to rapid progress."

The official "Statement," in dealing with the year 1887, states that, as compared with 1886, while there had been an increase of 1,203 miles of railway, or 9·35 per cent., there was a decrease in the gross earnings of £244,954, in silver, or 1·31 per cent.; an increase of £172,110, in silver, or 1·93 per cent., in the working expenses,—and thus, that the total net earnings showed a decrease of £417,064 (in silver), or no less than 4·27 per cent. This is a serious result; and I have heard that, while failure of crops and a lesser carriage of railway material have contributed, the lowering of rates on some of the railways under State management has had a pernicious effect on net revenue.

The total capital expended on Indian railways to the end of the year 1887 was £187,221,521, and the cost of the lines open averaged £13,000 a-mile; the least costly opened line being the Jodhpore, £1,843—and the most costly, the East Indian line, £21,483, per mile. The gross earning of all lines was £18,459,582; and the working expenses averaged 49 per cent.; the net revenue yielding a return of 5½ per cent. per annum on the capital cost. Still the State complains that it lost £2,267,800 (in silver) in 1887-8, by two causes: first, that the two guaranteed railways were entitled to one-half the surplus profits on their lines above 5 per cent., or £989,702 (Rx.); and second, because interest on guaranteed railway capital has to be paid in gold, while the earnings of the lines are realized in silver.

If in early days the Indian State had boldly made these, now, guaranteed railways on their own credit, about 25 per cent. more railway would have existed in India for the same annual outgoing for interest. Clearly it is the interest of every such country to raise its capital for expenditure, on permanent works, at the cheapest rate, which means on the best credit, which means, again, its own.

The Indian State began by guarantee at a high rate, and with division of profits over that high rate (of 5 per cent). In 1870 the policy of developing railways by the credit and under the charge of the State was inaugurated. In 1880-1 a recurrence to the system of aiding "private enterprise" took place: "assisted" railways. What the policy is now, I do not know. But it is obvious that the Indian State could raise railway loans in perpetuity, in gold, at 3, and on 99 years' terminal annuity at 3¼ per cent., or perhaps less. This is, at least, 1, to 1¼, per cent. less than would be demanded by "assisted" private enterprise; and to adopt the former, means that the State gets for the same annual charge more than 5 miles of railway if it finds its own money, and less than 3 in the case of "assisted" private enterprise.

I am told that guarantees, in gold, of 4 per cent. and a quarter of profits, of 4½ per cent., in gold, and of 4 per cent., in gold, with an addition of one quarter of net profits, have been given. If that be so, the State gets, clearly, much less line for its guarantee than it does for its own money. Who will defend this waste and loss?

It will thus be seen that I am opposed to any more tinkering at private enterprise, and advocate the extension of railways and other public works, also, in the most economical and efficient way, viz., by cheap capital, founded on the undoubted credit, of the State; and through the agency of the efficient and all-powerful and experienced executive of the State, rather than by the wasteful system of raising capital on indifferent credit, and by the weak and inefficient (in fact, totally inadequate) executives of the individuals and associations who pester the Indian State for concessions.

I want to see the whole benefit of the capital and property of the State going into the coffers of the State, which now, in many cases, gets a doubtful nibble, only, at its own cake.

But I feel it my duty, admiring as I do the Indian railway system, to express the opinion that in its working details it wants commercialising—if I may coin a word, to better express my meaning. The whole question of speed of trains wants reconsidering. In India the speed of trains is behind the age, and many of the regulations are too much like those of a military cantonment. I rode on the engine of one of the North Western lines, and going down, at a crawl, an incline of a mile or two of 1 in 50, I asked the driver, why? "Not allowed to go at more than ten miles an hour;" and, looking round, I saw a board with that announcement on it—"By order." At the bottom of this incline came an ascending gradient of 1 in 50, which we had to mount dead from the bottom, instead of getting the benefit of some extra velocity; all of which would have been left, in England or France, to the discretion of an experienced driver, such as was the man I rode with. This may be looked upon as a little matter of detail, but it is one of many straws which inclined me to think that there is too much military order about it all, and not enough individual authority.

At a station, which I need not name, a carriage, full of natives and their manifold bundles, pots, pans, baskets, pipes, sticks, and so on, was taken off, to be sent on by another train, to start some hours later. I asked, why? "Regulation that we are only to send on ten." "Bad gradient to place where those people are going"? "No, nearly flat." "Cannot the engine take the extra carriage?" "Oh! yes; but that is the regulation."

But before passing from such small things to great, let me say, that I look upon India as a source of supply, making us less and less dependent upon the protectionist United States. There is nothing in the United States—to which we at home pay £100,000,000 a-year for food and raw materials—which cannot, by proper organization, be produced better and cheaper in India—tobacco, sugar, cotton, petroleum, coal, wheat, maize, rice, raisins, all sorts of dried fruits, precious, and other, metals, and so on; while, amongst many other things, may be mentioned tea, coffee, varied tropical fruits, and the useful article of jute, which are on the Indian list of productions and not on that of the United States.

Again, India has the greatest advantage over the United States, in the abundant supply, and the cheapness and docility of its labour resources. But if India is, in the near future, to take some scores of the millions which are now paid to the protectionist United States, United States modes of cultivating the best quality of things, of rapid, through, transport, and of exchange, will have to be largely copied.

Now, while from Chicago, or any other emporium in the United States portion of North America, or from Montreal, or from any other big town or village in Canada, you can get a through bill of lading to Liverpool, London, or elsewhere, there is no such thing known in all India—save the recent experiment of Colonel Wallace from the port of Kurrachee, in connection with parts of the North Western State line, by an arrangement with the Hall, or Holt, line of steamers to Liverpool. To establish the United States system efficiently, the co-operation of all interests is essential, because the soul of the matter is a through rate: one single, moderate, and—in the case of such products as are sold to us by the United States—competing—charge throughout—combined with rapid transit and the best facilities for loading and discharge. I addressed the Secretary of State for India on this subject before I left England, and I have taken some pains to explain, in both railway and mercantile circles, the bearing of the through bill of lading on the competitions, and on the simple action and finance, of shipment and distribution. For such a purpose the whole railway system of India, in food and raw material districts, should be worked, for through rate purposes, as one. At present, I fear that system is, on the contrary, worked sectionally, if not, here and there, in antagonism. This is a great question.

And now for another great question. Wherever I went all over India, I asked, where are your elevators? and where are your public warehouses, in which every man, big or little, may deposit his grain, or his jute, or his rice, and take away an official receipt for his property?

I found that there was not an elevator in all India; and I could not trace the existence, at least, as a system, of public depôts. Every man his own "Godown," or warehouse.

I should here explain that the American elevator is a public depôt for grains, as well as a system of machinery by which grain can be "elevated" to floor levels, and shifted about with great rapidity, cheapness, and benefit to the grain itself. As respects the grain trade, our American cousins have developed theirs into a perfect system, and I never look at the vast, tall, wooden buildings at Montreal, New York, Chicago: everywhere—even amongst the growing villages on the Canadian Pacific Railway, where, a few years ago, there was nothing but the buffalo and the wandering Indian—without recognizing one of the finest phases of industrial progress. To Indian State officials, I say, "Go and see."

The elevator, I repeat, is not only machinery and a deposit warehouse, but, practically, a bank. The processes are various. The machinery—very much like a chain-pump, with small tin buckets on a band—takes up the grain from the trough, into which it is put out of bags, or from bulk, to the intended floor space, and then through a spout, which can be directed anywhere, it deposits the grain in the allotted space on the floor. If there is any fear of heating or mildew, the grain can be passed up and down, and the friction between grain and grain, in rapid passages, dries and brightens it, and at the same time gets rid of dust and rubbish. And when the grain is sent to market, the elevator machinery puts it into bags, or waggons, or anything, far better and more quickly than could be accomplished by manual labour. So far for the mechanical processes.

Now, one great obstacle to cheap storage and distribution is varying quality and separate ownerships. At our great grain warehouse, with seven acres of floor, at Grimsby, you find numbers of separate heaps; and often the wheat or barley heaps, laid side by side, are of exactly the same quality, though, because belonging to separate owners, kept apart. In the United States an independent State officer is appointed, whose duty it is to classify the grain into qualities. I forget the number of classes. I will assume it as six—it may be more or less. Well, you bring (say) 1,000 quarters of wheat to the great elevator of (say) Sturgis & Buckingham, at Chicago. The State officer certifies that it is of No. 1—or 2—or 3—or 4—or 5—or 6 class; and, accordingly, it is elevated to the floor, or portion of floor, containing the particular quality so numbered. Then you receive from Sturgis & Buckingham a small certificate, stating that you have deposited so much wheat, of such and such a number of quality. Thus, having put your property in safe custody, and got your receipt, you need take no further trouble. If you intend to keep it a while, paying a moderate monthly (I think) charge, and want money, any banker will lend you money on the deposit, or assignment of your receipt. On the contrary, if you prefer to keep your property, you can, at any time, at any city you may be staying at, sell your receipt at any Corn Exchange, and get your money, and have done with it.

I am not unmindful of objections in India to this mixing up your property with other people's. They had to be educated up to the common-sense of the matter, even in the United States, as since then they have been educated up to united dairies, and joint stock milk and cheese and butter factories. But assume that the producer is not ripe for so valuable, because so simple, a system, the elevator can still go on. All that would be needed would be more floor space. But I would point out the moral good of such a classification in leading to an emulation for improved quality, cleanness, &c. I am aware that the great merchants, who now make fortunes by buying locally the dirty grain, full of dust and stones, and sifting and cleaning it before bagging it for market, might object to through rates, elevators, and all; but the system must prevail, nevertheless. What I have written above applies to grain only. I may, however, mention that in many stations in America I have, in past times, seen husking machines for maize (Indian corn), at which any farmer could have his grain husked before transport; and I see no reason why Indian railways should not provide that, and many other facilities for trade, to the cultivator, at a moderate fixed rate.

I take it that what is wanted in India, especially, is—(1) more facilities for storage, transit, and loading and unloading; (2) places of secure deposit; (3) facilities for sifting, cleaning and drying; (4) in connection with the two latter, a system of certificates of deposit, on which the cultivator, or the dealer, could borrow money at the lowest rate, or sell at his pleasure, without having more to do than stamp and indorse over his certificate to the purchaser.

Now, if this system of deposit were adopted for grains, why not for jute, cotton, or any other product of India? And what is the objection, under a paternal Government, to the railways of India, the property of, or controlled by, the State, providing the warehouses, the machinery, and all the appliances required? To begin with, it would pay handsomely to do it. Then it would tend largely to develope the resources of the land in competition with competing nations; and, above all—and I ask this question with grave interest—would it not tend to relieve the poor cultivator from the grasp and tyranny of the bunia, the schroff, and the petty dealer? Again, would it not help the merchant, by providing him with storage for his local purchases; and might it not be made very useful in many districts, in time of scarcity or famine? for the tendency would always be to keep stocks of food, more or less, at each depôt station. Here is my suggestion, then, for whatever it may be worth.

Gauge.

Whoever proposed the 5 ft. 6 in. gauge for India, for Ceylon, for Canada, and the 5 ft. 3 in. for Ireland, or the 6 ft. gauge for the Erie Railway, was no friend to industrial mankind. Indian railways began amidst the smoke of the "War of Gauges"—the 7 ft. Great Western gauge of Brunel, as against the 4 ft. 8½ in. of the elder Stephenson: and I assume 5 ft. 6 in. was adopted in a spirit of compromise. It was certainly an experiment at the cost of the shareholders and the countries affected. The 7 ft.

gauge of Brunel has been largely obliterated on the Great Western, save that, for the sake of ancient history, it remains on a small portion of that noble railway, interwoven mostly with the 4 ft. 8½ in. in mixed gauge working. The whole of the 5 ft. 6 in. gauge lines have been taken up on the Grand Trunk lines in favour of 4 ft. 8½ in., and thus the Great Canadian line has become part and parcel, without change or break, of the whole railway system of the North American Continent. The Erie 6 ft. gauge has long since disappeared: and, when Ireland is physically connected with Scotland by a tunnel of something over twenty miles—as it can be at a cost of ten millions sterling—the 5 ft. 6 in. gauge will disappear by the time the first train runs through from Glasgow to Cork.

I went over the Ceylon 5 ft. 6 in. railway from Colombo, as far as Kandy; and my previous impressions of the absurdity of such a wide, expensive, and needless gauge were greatly strengthened. The line, too, winds about mountains, skirts their edges in a startling way—in one place you look down a perpendicular face of 1,500 feet upon the beautiful green of the young rice—and passes down to Kandy over a summit,—easily avoidable by using valleys full of industry, fertility, and traffic. But I remember that my old friend, Mr. George Wall, who has done more for the progress of Ceylon than any other man now living (and, who, by the way, in the Jubilee distribution of honours was wholly passed over, probably for that very reason), combatted the railway proposals of the day; but the Governor and his nominated Council carried their own way, and Ceylon has got about a-fifth less railway than it might have had, for the money expended, if using the world's gauge of 4 ft. 8½ in. This extravagance has, in India, been the parent of the metre gauge, and of narrower gauges still; and the evil of change and breaking bulk can only be mitigated by completing the metre gauge connections, where the length of metre gauge railway amounts to something like a system; by enlarging the narrower gauges to the metre gauge (39 inches) here and there; and, especially, by using, in dealing with important centres of traffic, the mixed gauge. The 5 ft. 6 in. gauge has certainly the advantage that a rail may be laid inside it, and thus the narrower vehicles may run through without impediment. This mixing of gauges would in Ceylon much cheapen future extensions, say, to Trincomalie, and other parts of the island now isolated for want of railway communication.

I may illustrate my meaning by giving one of my own experiences. The route between Darjeeling and Dhubri, on the Brahmaputra, is full of breaks. You travel on the Darjeeling line of 2 ft., or rather 1 ft. 11 in., gauge to Siligouri. From Siligouri to Parbatipur, and on to the Teista River, you have the "metre" gauge of 39 in. At the Teista you have to cross the river in a native boat to Darhla, from whence to Teista you have a 2 ft. 6 in. gauge. At Teista you go down and cross the river, again, in a native boat, to Darhla Ghat, whence again there is a 2 ft. 6 in. gauge; and from Darhla Ghat to Dhubri, 60 miles, you have a Government stern-wheel steamer. Coming upwards from Calcutta, you have to cross the river in a steamer at Sara Ghat, and to change trains. Such breaks and transhipments, on what is the mail route for the Brahmaputra ports and towns, and to Northern Assam, is so obstructive to travelling and interchange, that it is to be hoped that the Indian Government will make the gauge from Siligouri to Darhla Ghat uniform, and will arrange to cross the trains, or vehicles, over the rivers by adequate boats, as was, and is, done in many countries, should they find that the construction of bridges is too costly, or difficult, where shifting streams have to be dealt with.

Looking to the future, who will deny that before the end of the next quarter of a century India will be connected with England and with Europe by railways on the world's gauge? and, if so, it is not unreasonable to suppose that the uniformity introduced, at great cost, in England, in Canada, and in the United States, will force itself upon India, and that the 5 ft. 6 in. gauge will go "down among the dead men."

Railway Extension.

When the present Secretary for India took office, I took the liberty of long acquaintance to urge him to do a great work, which would redound alike to his credit and contribute in the most marked manner to the growth of Indian industries. At that time all articles of metal were at least ten per cent., all round, cheaper than they are at present. India wanted a fillip, and British industries were in that condition of stagnation out of which things do not start again without a push behind from some quarter or another. My advice was that he should prepare a project for his colleagues, under which the second stage of Indian Railway and other works should be accomplished in a period of five years, taking advantage of the unusually favourable conditions of low prices, and also of low freights,—conditions which probably would yield ten to fifteen per cent. more length of Railway for a lakh of rupees than might ever be achieved again. For the purpose of the completion of this second stage of development, I proposed that a hundred millions sterling be raised at, or under, three per cent.; and either on Imperial credit, with an Indian counter guarantee, or absolutely on Indian credit. I did not forget my often repeated advice, that such loans should be raised by way of terminable annuity, and not perpetual annuity, the term being the old-fashioned ninety-nine years, which period meant the assumed duration of the three stories of life, always existing together—the child, the parent, and the grand parent.

The noble Viscount had, I am convinced, the foresight and the courage of the occasion, but little was done. True, the Nagpore line—which opens out a good district, where grain has rotted for want of transport, while famine was decimating the people at no great distance from abundance—was commenced, and is now nearly completed for opening. This Railway will also give a short route between Bombay and Calcutta. The line completing the communication throughout, as between the Port of Rangoon and Mandalay, in Burmah, has also been opened; and the military lines on the North Western frontier, together with important works, such as the great Sukkur Bridge and others, have been proceeded with; but no distinct mark has been made.

One hundred millions sterling would make twenty thousand miles of new railway at five thousand pounds sterling a mile.

In his most interesting address, recently delivered at the Society of Arts, Sir Juland Danvers said, "There is no cause for boasting. More railways are required; and it is hoped that private enterprise will step in and provide what is wanted. Government has done much, but the taxes of the country cannot stand a larger demand upon them than they at present bear," &c. But the answer is—(a) That private enterprise will not "step in," except on wasteful terms, leading, I repeat, to India acquiring three miles of railway where she ought to get five at the same annual interest charge; (b) That if private enterprise did "step in," it would do so slowly, extravagantly, and on no single concentrated system; and (c) That, as a rule, what is called "private enterprise" in India has been, and always will be, a failure as contrasted with the combined action of the State, with its perfect credit and the thorough organization of its executive.

But, on the matter of taxation, to stop making railways, to help the Indian Budget, is simply suicidal. Sir Juland tells us that, while many lines were incomplete, and many others had been opened so recently that they were undeveloped, still, on the whole railway capital expenditure in 1887, a return of £5 : *2s.* 5*d.* per cent. was realised. Thus the outlay is a profitable investment. Assuming the future railways, which have been to a large extent planned and estimated for under the charge of the Indian Government, to do as well, the profit on the capital outlay would be the difference between, not exceeding three per cent. as the cost of the capital, and over £5 per cent. as the profit on the investment as such. But what would be the profit to India, to the Indian of every class, from the labourer upwards?

General Strachey has stated that the present Indian railways give a gain to the country of upwards of forty millions of pounds a-year.

Colonel Conway Gordon, the able Director-General of Indian Railways, says: "The whole history of Indian Railways is one long and *unsuccessful* attempt to get railways constructed without a State guarantee."

English doctrinaire "fads" do not fit Indian necessities.

The refusal to extend Indian Railways on the credit of the State is simply a refusal of a large profit on the investment itself, and a denial to the whole people of India of the far larger profit that investment would create and distribute.

But let us make one or two comparisons. Canada, with little over five millions of people, has over three-fourths as many miles of railway opened as the whole mileage of India and Burmah; and Canada, having tried private enterprise, has found the absolute necessity of State aid, in addition. The United States of America, with sixty millions of people, or a little over a-fifth of the population of India and Burmah, possessed, at the end of 1888, one hundred and forty-six thousand miles of railway. In America, thirteen thousand and eighty miles of railway were made and opened in the single year, 1887; as against the total of fourteen thousand eight hundred and ninety miles, which it has taken forty solid years in India to construct.

Is it surprising, then, that America has supplied the Mother Country and some of the Colonies with the corn, the meat, and the cotton which India, to the enrichment of her people, might have furnished!

I always expect to find "old womanism" in all administration of human affairs; simply because there is a class which "cannot dig, and to beg is ashamed"—who must, under the exigencies of party politics, be put into positions they are unfit to occupy; and while, as I honestly believe, the disease is not so bad in India as in Great Britain, it may be bad enough. I have on my table many papers about railway extensions from the Port of Kurrachee—which is four hundred miles nearer England than Bombay—and from the neglected port of Chittagong, leading into Upper Assam and Upper Burmah, and, in the future, to connect with China. Well, a Minute of the Government of India—dated Simla, August 25, 1887—strongly recommends the construction of a new system of railways from Chittagong to Badarpur, 253¾ miles; Laksham, Chandpur branch, 32 miles; Badarpur to Lumding, 115½ miles; Lumding to Makum, 213½ miles; Gonhatti branch, 110½ miles; Pilchar branch, 18 miles: total, 742 miles. And there can be no doubt that the construction of this system of lines, at a cost of

£6,505,000 (Rs. x), would be profitable as an investment, made with cheap Government credit and cash, and would bring to the State and people development, security, and peace. No doubt whatever. "But," the Government Minute goes on, "fully as the Government of India recognizes the importance of opening up by railway the tracts of Eastern Bengal and Assam, now in question, they are not in a financial position which would justify the offer of a guarantee *for a purely commercial* railway, and must, therefore, adhere to the decision of January, 1883 [*now between six and seven years ago, with nothing done*], by which the project was classed in Schedule B., and can receive no aid from the State beyond such as is comprised in a concession under what are known as Bengal and North Western terms." Now, what is the pith and the arithmetic of all this? It is admitted that this system of railways is most essential. But it is stated that the Government is "not in a financial position which would justify the offer of a guarantee for a purely commercial railway." The "purely commercial" railway pays: the purely military railway does not. Therefore Government is in a financial position to construct the latter, but not the former.

Going back and applying the figures preceding, the arithmetic would be this: had the Indian Government gone ahead over six years ago and done the work with their own 3 per cent. capital, they might have made a profit of over 2 per cent. on £6,505,000 = in six years to nearly a million: and the people, applying the figures stated of the profit in development and general benefit, would have received, all round (as £40,000,000 is to an outlay of £182,879,655) = about £7,500,000, on an outlay of £6,505,000 for (say) six years, plus compound profit. I give the figures as I have received them. I see little to object to in them; but if they are approximate in the slightest degree what are we to say about the Simla Minute?

I question the entire exactness of the division of "military," and "purely commercial" railways. It is, no doubt, a question of degree; but, in principle, every railway must serve all purposes, more or less. But the "commercial" railway is assumed to be eminently remunerative, while the military is not. Thus the Simla Minute assumes that "private enterprise" is to do what will pay, and the State what will not pay.

It will be observed that the rough estimates above assume that six years of benefit have been wiped out, and tend to show the loss by the delay.

The, undeniable, advance of the wages of labour, is no small portion of this profit to the people, of £40,000,000 annually.

If the reader will consult the Appendix to the "Final Report of the Royal Commission on Gold and Silver," he will find a table showing the average wages of agricultural and skilled labour in selected districts of India and Burmah. Excluding Burmah and sea-ports—where wages are abnormally high—the average wages where the country has been opened up are, for common labourers 59 rupees per annum, and for skilled labourers 152 rupees per annum, as compared with the calculation of Mr. Barbour, the Financial Secretary, in 1882, of 27 rupees per annum.

NOTE.—Five years ago, when India had less than 11,000 miles of railway, General Strachey, the highest authority, probably, when asked whether the construction of railways in India had increased the value of land so far as to enable the people to more easily contribute the taxes they have to pay, replied: "Certainly. The relief to the country is immense. The saving to the people of India is, probably, twice the gross income received by the railway companies.

It is a very large sum indeed; it amounts to £30,000,000 or £40,000,000, probably, *annually*." Thus, in 1888-9, with nearly 15,000 miles of railway, against 11,000, the people's gain must be over the £40,000,000 I have assumed, above. But, at the Society of Arts, Sir Charles Bernard, now Revenue Secretary at the India Office, said: "The Government of India is often taunted with having directly lost forty millions sterling on the whole railway account in the last thirty years. I do not hesitate to say that the people of India have benefited, every year, to that extent by the introduction of railways in that country."

COMPARATIVE RATES of Carriage, by Railway, in INDIA and the UNITED STATES.

It is very difficult to contrast the rates and fares on United States and on Indian railways. There is the difference of currency, the difference of weights and measures; and the drawbacks, transit combinations and rings in America; dollars and cents are one thing; rupees, annas and pies, quite another. Then there is the "maund" in India, and the 100 lbs. with 2,000 lbs. to a ton—and not 2,240 lbs. as in England—in the United States. Then the circumstances of the people, as regards passenger travelling, in the two countries are totally dissimilar.

Thus, I should have been in despair in trying to make even an approximate contrast, if my kind friend and old acquaintance, Mr. T. W. Wood, of the Bombay and Baroda Railway, had not given the following information:—

45, Finsbury Circus,
London, E.C.
6th April, 1889.

My Dear Sir Edward,

I have pleasure in enclosing two Statements, prepared on the same basis, giving some selected long distance actual rates for railway carriage of main descriptions of produce or manufacture now in force in India. The one marked (A) relates to this Company's system; the other, marked (B), relating to the East Indian Railway, and furnished to me for communication to you by my friend, Mr. Dunstan, the Secretary of that Company.

These Statements will, I hope, supply you with the information you wish for, as regards India, in an authentic shape.

I wish I could give you similarly authentic particulars as regards American rates, but I have no reliable or sufficient details.

Poor's Manual for 1886 states, however, that for the year 1885 the averages on 123,110 miles operated by *American* (U.S.) Railroad Companies were as follows, viz.:—

	cents
Per *passenger* per mile	2·198
Per ton (2,000 lbs.) of *goods* per mile	1·057

Now, Conway Gordon's Report on *Indian* Railways for 1887 indicates (see para. 12, Chap. VIII., page 98, Part I.), dividing receipts by mileages of units, that the average receipts on 13,578 miles worked were as follows, viz.:—

	pies
Per passenger per mile	2·50
Per ton of goods (2,240 lbs.) per mile	7·17

These average rates represent, taking the rupee as = 1*s.* 5*d.* sterling, and the dollar as = 4*s.* sterling—

For passengers, an average receipt per mile of { 0·23 pence, or 0·48 cents,

this being little more than one-fifth of the average American charge—

For goods, an average receipt per ton of 2,000 lbs., of, say, per mile .... { 0·57 pence, or 1·19 cents,

this being about 12½ per cent. more than the average American charge.

The Statements I enclose show that main staples of Indian agricultural produce are carried at much lower rates than the averages quoted.

Believe me,
My dear Sir Edward,
Sincerely yours,
T. W. WOOD.

SIR E. W. WATKIN, BART., M.P.

(A)

BOMBAY, BARODA, AND CENTRAL INDIA RAILWAY (includes the Rajputana State Railway, the Holkar State Railway, the Sindia-Neemuch State Railway, the Ruoari-Ferozepore State Railway, and the Cawnpore-Achnera State Railway).

LONG DISTANCE RATES.

March, 1889.

Exchange, 1*s.* 5*d. the rupee; one ton* = 2,000 *lbs.*

T.S. means transhipment at Sabarmati from one gauge to another.

WHEAT.

Delhi to Bombay, T.S. 888 miles.
10*as.* 9*p.* per maund = *Rs.*16 : 5*as.* 3*p.* per ton.
= £1 : 3*s.* 1½*d.* per ton, or ·312*d.* per ton mile.

Cawnpore to Bombay, T.S. 1,071 miles.
*Rs.*79 : 2*as.* 8*p.* per 100 maunds = *Rs.*19 : 3*as.* 10*p.* per ton.
= £1 : 7*s.* 3*d.* per ton, or ·305*d.* per ton mile.

FOOD GRAINS (other than wheat, including rice).

Delhi to Bombay, T.S. 888 miles.
11*as.* per maund = *Rs.*16 : 11*as.* 4*p.* per ton.
= £1 : 3*s.* 8*d.* per ton, or ·319*d.* per ton mile.

Cawnpore to Bombay, T.S. 1,071 miles.
*Rs.*79 : 11*as.* per 100 maunds = *Rs.*19 : 5*as.* 11*p.* per ton.
= £1 : 7*s.* 5¼*d.* per ton, or ·307*d.* per ton mile.

COMMON SEEDS (including oil seeds).

Cawnpore to Bombay, T.S. 1,071 miles.
11*as.* per maund = *Rs.*16 : 11*as.* 4*p.* per ton.
= £1 : 3*s.* 8*d.* per ton, or ·265*d.* per ton mile.

SALT.

Kharaghoda to Bombay, 371 miles.
8*as.* per maund = *Rs.*12 : 2*as.* 5*p.* per ton.
= 17*s.* 2½*d.* per ton, or ·556*d.* per ton mile.

Kharaghoda to Cawnpore, T.S. 818 miles.
*Rs.*74 : 6*as.* 8*p.* per 100 maunds = *Rs.*18 : 1*as.* 5*p.* per ton.
= £1 : 5*s.* 7½*d.* per ton, or ·375*d.* per ton mile.

Kharaghoda to Agra, T.S. 594 miles.
10*as.* 5*p.* per maund = *Rs.*15 : 13*as.* 2*p.* per ton.
= £1 : 2*s.* 5*d.* per ton, or ·452*d.* per ton mile.

SUGAR.

Bombay, for distances over 800 *miles*, T.S.

¼*p*. per maund per mile = *Rs*.25 : 5*as*. 1*p*. per ton.
(for 800 miles)
= £1 : 15*s*. 10½*d*. per ton, or ·537*d*. per ton mile.

COTTON.

(1) *Full-pressed*, i. e., *more than* 24 *lbs. per cubic foot.*

Broach to Bombay, 202 miles.

4*as*. 1*p*. per maund = *Rs*.6 : 3*as*. 3*p*. per ton.
= 8*s*. 9*d*. per ton, or ·519*d*. per ton mile.

Wudwan to Bombay, 377 miles.

8*as*. 10*p*. per maund = *Rs*.13 : 6*as*. 8*p*. per ton.
= 19*s*. per ton, or ·604*d*. per ton mile.

(2) *Half-pressed*, i. e., 6 *to* 11 *lbs. per cubic foot.*

Broach to Bombay, 202 miles.

7*as*. 1*p*. per maund = *Rs*.10 : 12*as*. 2*p*. per ton.
= 15*s*. 3*d*. per ton, or ·905*d*. per ton mile.

Wudwan to Bombay, 377 miles.

11*as*. 9*p*. per maund = *Rs*.17 : 13*as*. 7*p*. per ton.
= £1 : 5*s*. 3½*d*. per ton, or ·805*d*. per ton mile.

(3) *Three-quarter pressed*, i. e., *between* 11 *and* 24 *lbs. per cubic foot, carried at approximately proportionate intermediate rates.*

PIECE GOODS, yarn and twist (in bales).

Bombay to Agra, T.S. 847 miles.

Rs.2 : 3*as*. 1*p*. per maund = *Rs*.53 : 4*as*. 8*p*. per ton.
= £3 : 15*s*. 6*d*. per ton, or 1·069*d*. per ton mile.

Bombay to Delhi, T.S. 888 miles.

Rs.2 : 6*as*. 7*p*. per maund = *Rs*.58 : 9*as*. 9*p*. per ton.
= £4 : 3*s*. 0¼*d*. per ton, or 1·121*d*. per ton mile.

Bombay to Cawnpore, T.S. 1,071 miles.

Rs.222 : 4*as*. per 100 maunds = *Rs*.54 : 0*as*. 3*p*. per ton.
= £3 : 16*s*. 6¼*d*. per ton, or ·857*d*. per ton mile.

COAL.

Bombay to Wudwan, 377 miles.

5*as*. 11*p*. per maund = *Rs*.8 : 15*as*. 10*p*. per ton.
= £0 : 12*s*. 9*d*. per ton, or ·405 per ton mile.

IRON AND STEEL.

Bombay to Delhi, T.S. 888 miles.

14*as*. 8*p*. per maund = *Rs*.22 : 4*as*. 6*p*. per ton.
= £1 : 11*s*. 6¾*d*. per ton, or ·426*d*. per ton mile.

TIMBER (unwrought).
Bombay to Wudwan, 377 miles.
7as. per maund = *Rs.*10 : 10*as.* 1*p.* per ton.
= £0 : 15*s.* 0¾*d.* per ton, or ·479*d.* per ton mile.

KEROSINE OIL.
Bombay to Delhi, T.S. 888 miles.
*Rs.*1 : 3*as.* 6*p.* per maund = *Rs.*29 : 9*as.* 11*p.* per ton.
= £2 : 1*s.* 11½*d.* per ton, or ·567*d.* per ton mile.

T. W. W.

45, FINSBURY CIRCUS, E.C.,
6th April, 1889.

(B)

EAST INDIAN RAILWAY.

LONG DISTANCE RATES.

February, 1889.

Exchange, 1*s.* 5*d.* *the rupee; one ton* = 2,000 *lbs.*

WHEAT, EDIBLE GRAINS, SEEDS, &c.
Delhi to Howrah, 954 miles.
*Rs.*53 per 100 maunds = *Rs.*12 : 14*as.* 1*p.* per ton.
= 18*s.* 3*d.* per ton, or ·229*d.* per ton mile.

COTTON AND WOOL (from Saharunpur and beyond).
Ghaziabad to Howrah, 941 miles.
*Rs.*4 : 0*as.* 9*p.* per bale of 300 lbs. (pressed to not less than 43 lbs. per c. foot). } = *Rs.*26 : 15*as.* 8*p.* per ton.
= £1 : 18*s.* 2½*d.* per ton, or ·487*d.* per ton mile.

COAL.
Gerideh to Delhi, 795 miles.
*Rs.*58 per 100 maunds = *Rs.*14 : 1*as.* 6*p.* per ton.
= 19*s.* 11¾*d.* per ton, or ·301*d.* per ton mile.

SALT.
Howrah to Cawnpore, 684 miles.
*Rs.*45 per 100 maunds = *Rs.*10 : 15*as.* 0*p.* per ton.
= 15*s.* 6*d.* per ton, or ·272*d.* per ton mile.

PIECE GOODS.

Howrah to viâ Jubbulpore, 784 miles.

*Rs.*165 per 100 maunds = *Rs.*40 : 1*as.* 7*p.* per ton.

= £2 : 16*s.* 9¾*d.* per ton, or ·87*d.* per ton mile.

IRON, STEEL, SPELTER, AND ZINC.

Howrah to Delhi, 954 miles.

*Rs.*80 per 100 maunds = *Rs.*19 : 7*as.* 1*p.* per ton.

= £1 : 7*s.* 6*d.* per ton, or ·346*d.* per ton mile.

KEROSINE (for Saharunpur and beyond).

Howrah to viâ Ghaziabad, 941 miles.

*Rs.*79 : 4*as.* per 100 maunds = *Rs.*19 : 4*as.* 2*p.* per ton.

= £1 : 7*s.* 3¼*d.* per ton, or ·348*d.* per ton mile.

These rates must be taken as the mileage earnings on the railways; and the cost of bringing the traffic to and taking it from the stations must be added. Then contrasting Indian with United States rates, it must be remembered that, while Indian rates, under the present system of management, are very difficult to alter, our American cousins do not hesitate in competition to "cut" rates. Then the extraordinary facilities for loading, unloading, and warehousing in the United States is in itself a reduction of price. Indian rates and Indian methods are not yet framed to meet United States competition.

PETROLEUM FINDING IN INDIA.

It came to the knowledge of, I believe, Sir R. Sandeman, that the camels passing through the country near Quetta appeared very frequently with their noses, heads, and other parts of their bodies blackened by what appeared to be petroleum; and it was found that, for time out of mind, this black stuff, whatever it might be, had been used by the camel drivers as a cure for mange and scurvy, and to heal wounds caused by the friction of harness. The drivers, when appealed to, showed the places—black oozes out of the ground and rocks—where they gathered the substance. This led to inquiry and prospecting, and Lord Dufferin having appealed to Lord Lansdowne, in Canada, a very able and experienced Canadian, known also, I believe, to Lord Dufferin himself, was set to work to report on these "finds."

His report is a public document, and I have a print of it now before me. It is dated "Simla, September 10, 1887," is addressed "To the Secretary to the Government of India, Public Works Department," and signed "R. A. Townsend, Superintendent, Petroleum Works, Beluchistan." The report begins thus: "At several places in the Rawal Pindi plateau, in the North Punjaub, petroleum makes its appearance, saturating sandstones, shales, and limestones of tertiary age, with little or no surface accumulations; and it may be seen in small quantities upon the waters of sulphurous springs."

After describing the various "finds" in detail, the report says:—"The ease with which this supposed oil-field can be reached—the North Western Railway skirting it for miles—the favourable lay of the land, over long wide valleys, the question of fuel, water, labour and food supplies, and character of climate, place it in great contrast with others known to me, where there is a probability of obtaining petroleum in quantity." Again, "Colonel Lovett has, against hostile criticism, steadily maintained his faith in petroleum being obtained in quantities in his district; and he and Mr. Blackburn have recently conducted boring operations at Fatehgung, with poor appliances, in the hope of getting sufficient crude oil to supply Rawal Pindi with gas: let us hope they may not be disappointed."

Colonel Lovett is the district engineer of the State, just returned from the Black Mountain war, where his sword-sheath was struck by a musket-ball, which just missed his body. Mr. Blackburn is the engineer of the petroleum gas-works at Rawal Pindi, which supply the cantonments there. He is an "Owens College" man of great promise.

The report concludes:—"To one who for years has sought, and found, oily fluid in its jungle fastnesses and in some dark and ugly corners of the earth, there comes at this stage the temptation to make the wish the father to the thought, and to recommend, without hesitation, costly and extensive trial borings over the Rawal Pindi plateau, which, by comparison, is so fair a land and so easy of access: but this I am not prepared to do, for, notwithstanding fine shows, and many of them, the element of uncertainty, in testing for large deposits of petroleum, is a constant attendant upon the wisest and most experienced among oil miners, even with the addition of a geological knowledge pertaining to such work. But a steam engine and considerable plant is already in the field at Rawal Pindi, and in view of the many and good shows which mark the rocks at the surface, after climbing through, perhaps, hundreds of feet of strata, and in view of the great value to the Punjaub in particular, and to India as a whole, which a large production of an excellent quality of oil would be, I think it a pity to let the question of oil or no oil, in the North Punjaub, remain much longer an unsolved problem. The adventurous miner of America would sniff the oil shows, which I have seen during the past month, with mental visions of derricks, tanks, pipe-lines, and refineries in the near future, and would give it a trial were it in any other country than far-off India."

I have also another public document before me: a report "dated Simla, the 14th September, 1888.—From R. A. Townsend, Superintendent of Petroleum Works, Beluchistan, to the Secretary to the Government of India, Public Works Department, Simla." It begins: "I have the honour to submit the following report of a recent examination of the petroleum deposits in the Upper Assam Valley, made by orders of the Government of India;" and while it is a very full and clear exposition of what the writer saw and of his views thereon, I will merely quote one or two extracts, as the pith of the document:—

"Throughout these hills (Tippam), so far as examined, the oil shows are abundant, and of the most surprising character. The sandstones bordering the chief nallas are dripping with oil; the loose sand in the stream-beds is so charged with it in places that a hole made with a walking-stick is immediately filled, and if a handful of sand be squeezed, it parts with its oil as a sponge with water. Numerous holes on the hill-sides are half filled with oil, mud, leaves, &c.; and there are places so charged with oil vapour, or gases, as to be unpleasant to one unaccustomed to the fumes of an oil refinery. Nowhere have I seen such shows of oil in a state of nature; they are not confined to one or two isolated places, but extend for miles continuously, every hill-side and nalla being more or less marked by its presence."

"For want of time I did not undertake an examination of the vast tract of country to the south-east of Jaipur, known to contain shows of petroleum along the northern border of the Nagas, and far up the valleys within them. I believe them to be very like those of the Makum district, but I cannot speak of their value without a careful examination, further than to say, that they, together with other shows, found in water-wells on many tea plantations—such as at Bazalona and Talup, far out in the plains—stamp the country in which they appear as being in connection with and a continuation of the Makum area, and that collectively they are an index to an oil deposit of vast extent and probably of surprising richness."

These are the observations of an experienced and able explorer, evidently endeavouring in vain to induce the Indian Government to prove the extent and value of their own property by their own executive organizations.

Stumbling by mere chance upon another public document: it is "dated 23 March, 1888," and docketed—"The Secretary of State for India in Council, and John d'Oyly Noble, Esq.—Agreement."

Rumour has it that this Mr. Noble came from Canada with Mr. Townsend, and managed to get this agreement made in his own name. But I have only to deal with the agreement as I find it.

The agreement recites that all earth oil is, by the Punjaub Land Revenue Act, 1887, "deemed to be the property of the Government," and that "it is competent to the Government to assign and make over the right to search for and extract earth oil." Then the agreement stipulates (Clause 1): "On and from the 1st day of January, 1888, until the 31st December, 1890, inclusive, or until the contractor has selected, in the manner hereafter in this article provided, five blocks of land in the area and for the purposes in this article described, whichever may first happen," that "the contractor (Noble) shall enjoy the exclusive right of prospecting for earth oil throughout the whole of the Punjaub as now existing, north and west of a line drawn from the town of Jammu to the town of Sialcot, thence following the line of the railway viâ Wazirabad, Lala Musa, Pind Dadan Khan, and Kundian to Khoawar, and from the last-named place due west to the Western frontier of the Punjaub." A reference to the map will show the excessive area of this "exclusive right" of prospecting.

Then the "blocks" may "be less than, but shall not exceed, five in number," and they "shall be square, with sides each four miles long, each block amounting to 16 square miles in total area." That is, the contractor has the "exclusive right" to find out the best and richest sites, and then may select 80 square miles of such best sites. The acreage is 51,200 acres.

Clause 4 stipulates that the contractor "shall immediately after the execution of this agreement proceed to Canada, and shall bring out with all despatch to the area specified in Article 1. . . . machinery, tools, skilled mechanics, and all other necessary machinery and appliances, sufficient for the purpose of effectively prosecuting his search for earth oil with all due diligence and despatch, and shall put down, to a depth of 500 feet each, not less than 10 wells in the area specified in Article 1 before the expiration of the period referred to in the said article."

I cannot find that Mr. Noble has complied with this clause, so far—but he may be doing so.

Then by Clause 7: "The Government agrees . . . . to buy from the contractor during a term of five years, at a fixed rate of 11 Rs. 4a. 3p. per cwt., whatever quantity of lubricating oil may from time to time be required by the North Western Railway, and not in any case less than 804 tons per annum. The said oil to be delivered in bulk by the contractor into tank-wagons of the said railway, &c."

The price named is £22 : 10*s*. a ton, in silver, or £18,090 per annum, minimum, or a total purchase by the Indian Government equal to £90,450, in silver, in the five years. The price deserves criticism.

Then, "The Government agrees to transport, during a period of five years, over all Indian railways worked by the State, any quantity of earth oil extracted from wells sunk under this agreement, and of products manufactured by the contractor . . . . at the uniform rate of one quarter pie per maund (82 lbs.) per mile in the case of consignments of full wagon-loads."

No land taxes are to be levied on the contractor.

Clause 11 stipulates that the royalty receivable by the Government, "by way of land revenue or rent," shall be "the value of one-twentieth part (calculated at the rate of three rupees for every 315 pounds weight of crude earth oil)," &c.

Clause 16 stipulates that "The contractor shall not nor will assign, sub-let, or otherwise transfer or dispose of the rights and privileges conferred by this agreement, save with the written consent of the Government first had and obtained."

Clause 5 is peculiar:

"For every well up to, but not exceeding, a maximum of ten in all, sunk by the contractor for the purpose of prospecting only, and previously to the selection by him of the blocks of land hereinbefore in Article 1 of this agreement referred to, to the depth of five hundred feet or more, below the level of the ground, which does not produce earth oil in remunerative quantities, and is, consequently, abandoned by him, the Government will (but subject always to the proviso hereinafter in this article contained) pay to him the sum of Rs. 2,500 on account of each such well so abandoned: *Provided always*, that nothing shall be payable by the Government to the contractor on account of any such well, unless and until he shall have filled up such, and shall have removed any obstructions which he may have placed in, on, or near the same; and the contractor hereby binds himself to fill up all such wells so abandoned, and to remove all such obstructions in, on, or near the same."

Now, I simply ask what the Government has got, or can get, by thus giving a monopoly of discovery to Mr. Noble? I may be told that Mr. Noble's "blocks" are "alternate;" so that a spare block will always be between his blocks. I have little doubt that this agreement was made in the despair of the Indian Executive of getting any better means sanctioned under the shadow of "private enterprise." We must try to change all this.

INDIAN "PRIVATE ENTERPRISE," AND THE NON-DEVELOPMENT OF INDIAN RESOURCES.

I NEVER like to be knocked down by such phrases as "individual effort," "private enterprise," and so on. The individual, and the co-operation of individuals, have functions, no doubt, and great ones. But they do not possess the vast powers of the State. And thus, when State work is handed over to "private enterprise"—usually with some job at the back of it—there is a muddle and a mess. So it will always be.

Private enterprise—meaning the action of individuals, or the association of individuals unassisted by guarantees, special privileges, or adequate grants in aid—has, it seems to me, been a costly failure in India. It has been a mistake—as respects irrigation works, railways, docks, and harbours, the getting and working of minerals, and so on—to rely upon it. It is true that spinning and weaving companies in cotton, and in jute, cotton press companies, and other such organizations, employing the cheap and sharp labour of the country, have done fairly well. It is true that one or two manufacturers have left England and set up mills in India, and have made fortunes, free from hostile legislation and trade-unions. Cawnpore may be cited as a good example; and its boot and shoe factory, where little children take stitching and other piece-work, and employ as subs lesser children at small pittances, to aid them—is very interesting proof of the attraction of regular work with regular money wages to all child-kind in India. Such industries are local and domestic: no doubt they will spread, there is plenty of room; and freedom from factory inspectors and strikes for wages—at least at present—are valuable. People in England often forget that the Government of India is paternal: and that when it ceases to be so, it will cease altogether—so far as the Sovereign and people of England are concerned. How the Statesmen of such a Government can, even now, call out for "private enterprise" to come into their parlour and make great public works—as, for example, the railways of 720 miles, needed to open out Assam by the Chittagong, Cachar and Dibrughar, and the Goalunda routes, with any expectation of present or future success (except by paying through the nose),—is past my understanding. They know well that they never have, and never will, to the world's end, raise money on bad credit as well as on good. They know that the Government credit always brings the cheapest money, and the largest native investments. They forget the deterring effect on the confidence of capital of these annual meetings of delegates, where combination and treason-talk is permitted, and the day of native rule over English people, and their property, predicted. They ought to know that almost everything within the range above defined, hitherto committed to "private enterprise," has either had to be bought back again, or is now languishing in the littleness of its results. And what is the consequence? why, that enlargement of the means of transport, and extension of irrigation, and docks and harbours, go on at snails-paces; and that the "development of the vast mineral resources" of India has no existence whatever—while the Indian Government is waiting for the moon to come to bed to them.

Fifty years ago it was known to the Indian Government that wonderful deposits of coal existed in Assam: notably, around and south of Makum, in the extreme north-east of the English boundary,—as well as in other districts, such as Shillong, for instance. Some eight or nine years ago "private enterprise," in the persons of a Calcutta firm of merchants (since in dissolution, I hear, got a "concession" from the Indian Government of 30 square miles of coal land, and of the coal and petroleum in it, in the north-east of Assam. This "private enterprise" sold its rights for a "consideration" to a London Company: that London Company has spent £720,000 on 87 miles of railway and in opening up the coal, and has parted with a few hundreds to refine the petroleum found in 1863 by Mr. Metcalf—who had to abandon his efforts for want of capital and of transport,—and in poking about in two other places.

This company—"private enterprise"—after raising money in all sorts of ways, and being put to great straits, earns about 1 per cent. on its capital, to which must be added an annual "Lakh," as subsidy from India, now reduced to £7,200 in gold in London, by reason of the depreciation in silver (almost all of which is absorbed in paying high interest upon its debenture debts). The "royalty" paid by the company on coal sent to market is three annas a ton, in silver, or fourpence half-penny in silver, or about threepence in gold. The largest get of coal, according to the company's last report, for the year 1887, was 87,000 tons, on which the royalty in silver would be £1,630, as against the subsidy of a lakh, or £10,000 in silver. So much for the profit and loss account, as between the Indian Government and "private enterprise" in Assam. The account would be more unsatisfactory still if past years', greater, losses were totalled up. But the account as between the industrial and other interests of India and "private enterprise" is summed up thus: the Indian taxpayer has been paying thousands a year in subsidies, yet the coal—existing in abundance and most easily worked—has not been got out of the ground and sent to market in any adequate quantity. When I was at Dibrughar, I saw about 50,000 tons of this really fine coal lying in stacks on the sandy, muddy shore—the "private enterprise" directors in London having forbidden its sale to a steamship company trading up there who wanted it, because of some quarrel between that steamship company and another steamship company—each controlled by a leading Scotchman—into which quarrel "private enterprise" had foolishly, and needlessly been thrown.

Then, as to petroleum, which, so far as the Government agent's practical opinion goes, lies up there in boundless quantity—not a physic-bottleful has been sent to market after all these years under this "private enterprise." The date of the original concession was May, 1880.

There are plenty of parallels. In the above case, "private enterprise" has fought against great odds and vast difficulties. It has opened a highway into a wilderness. Maybe, in time, it will get its money back. But the great purpose of quickly and thoroughly developing the production of coal and petroleum in the wonderful district of North Assam is too big for "private enterprise;" and "private enterprise" has merely kept out the energy of the State.

The "Statement exhibiting the moral and material progress and condition of India during the year 1886-7, 23rd number"—ordered by the House of Commons to be printed 10th August, 1888—throws a deal of light on this "private enterprise" business, though it hides a good deal. For instance, no statement of the royalties paid, and services done, by "private enterprise" is given, under any "head."

Under the head of "Mines and Mineral Resources" (p. 2107), it is therein recorded:—"Out of 105 collieries, there were 69 at work during the year. They employed 24,794 hands, as compared with 22,745 in the previous year: and the total output of coal rose from 1,294,221 tons to 1,388,487 tons. The total imports of coal from Europe and Australia during the year were 765,668 tons." Now, as the East India and other Railways are the owners and workers of coal-mines for their large and increasing working consumption, I can understand where the increase over 1884-5 has come from. Certainly, where "private enterprise," in the main, has got concessions for 105 collieries, and only works 69 of them, development cannot be going on very fast. But it must be remembered that coal has been mined and carried along the great rivers and railways of India for, certainly, a generation; and yet the total output is less than one-eightieth of the output of the coal areas of England, Wales, and Scotland.

So much for coal. Now for iron. This Blue Book says:—

"Iron is worked to a limited extent, after native methods, in all provinces, and in many districts. The Barrakur Ironworks, which have, within a radius of five miles, excellent coal, iron, and lime, did not pay anything during the year: the stock of pig-iron rose from 677 tons to 3,683 tons, and there were few buyers." Now this iron-works was "private enterprise," which failed; and then the Government took it in hand, and, apparently, has made a mess of it, for want of a proper practical staff, and by grudging the capital necessary to enable a trade to be conducted large enough to pay.

But I return to petroleum. This Blue Book says:—"The companies working petroleum on the Arakan coast have failed, and earth oil, there, is raised only by native workers on a limited scale. The Upper Burma oil-field, near Tenangyoung, is being prospected, and the old oil wells are being worked under the same system as under the Burmese rule. The oil is brought down to Rangoon, to a refinery. It yields a comparatively small proportion of burning oil, and the industry is not at present flourishing. At the end of the year (1887) the Khatun oil-field in Baluchistan was still being investigated; and it is hoped that it may pay to burn this oil in locomotives on the Quetta Railway."

So much for a product, of which there is probably more in the various regions of India than in all the United States or Russia. But I will return to this (Sibi) oil-find hereafter.

Now for copper. The Blue Book says: "Though copper ore is found in many parts of India, and was worked in old times, and though some little copper is still worked in Rajputana, nearly all the copper used in India comes now from Europe, China, and Australia."

Then as to lead, "Lead is found in great quantities: but the company joined to work the rich lead mines of Tenasserim was at a standstill, and the only lead workings, of which report was made during 1886-7, were the mines in the Shan States, some of which were visited by an officer of the Geological Survey."

The next quotation is as to tin: "Tin is produced by Chinese miners in the south of the province of Tenasserim; but the Mergui mines are not nearly so productive as tin mines further down the Malay peninsula."

I give next (p. 108) all that affects British India as to gold:—"No gold sources, except river sand, yielding a very poor out-turn, as with gold workings in Continental India, have yet been discovered in Upper Burma." The report says of the Mysore State:—"Altogether five mines are returned as having been worked in Mysore and the Madras Presidency. Only one company is said to be in a flourishing condition, and the Mysore Government report the output of that company to be about 2,000 ounces a month. Though extensive areas have been granted for gold mining in Mysore, actual mining operations have been carried on only in a very small and insignificant proportion of the areas taken up; and in no case has the work been carried on by the applicants for the grant themselves." So much for "private enterprise" and gold grants.

Then as to silver: "The only silver mining of which report has been made is the extraction of silver from lead works in the Shan Hills. Many silver mines are reported to exist in the Shan Hills; but, as yet, only one or two sites on the western edge of the Shan States have been visited."

"Visited" by whom? I regret I cannot find, so far, anywhere, reports as to the perennial visits and the doings of the "officers of the Geological Survey." I was told that one of them said of a place, where coal has since been found in abundance, that "if ever coal were found there he would eat it." Has he done so?

What is wanted is the experienced miner, and deep borings systematically made, and not mere theorists in geology. A system of rewards for native "findings" would operate well.

The Russian Government at Bakou are developing their vast petroleum supplies, and already they are competitors of growing importance with the United States and Canada, even in the Indian markets; and had the Indian Government shown a tithe of the energy displayed by Russia, Indian petroleum might by this time have shared the whole trade, with a fair prospect of providing the bulk of Indian supply, hereafter.

An interesting article, the work of a Russian engineer, appeared in the "Revue des deux Mondes," last October. I recommend it to the perusal of all who care about the subject, and I translate the following short extract. I may premise by stating that the production of petroleum in the United States and Canada, in 1884, was 3,023,253 tons; and it was probably 4,000,000 tons in 1888, a quantity which, at the price per ton agreed to be paid by the Indian Government to Mr. Noble, as shown on page 48, would be worth £90,000,000, in silver.

"In comparing the Russian official reports with those of the United States, the annual production of the latter would be about double that of Russia. The proportion would even be greater—approaching three-fold—in favour of the United States, if we admit the approximate estimates of M. Hue, who brings the annual production of the United States up to 5,376 millions, and those of Russia up to 1,954 millions, of kilogrammes. (Bakou, 1,932,000,000; Caucasia, 6,720,000; and Transcaucasia, 15,624,000, kilogrammes.) It would result from this that Bakou supplies very nearly the total of the annual production, since *its figure quantity* is more than 80 times above that of all the other Russian localities put together. But the district of Bakou, even including all the peninsula of Apcheron, has only an area of 1,828 kilometres square, of which a portion only has been worked; it will be seen, therefore, how the producing power of the United States is inferior to that of Bakou in the light of the proportion between the product and the extent of territory which furnishes it. In fact, that of the United States being 921,355 kilometres square, or five hundred times the extent of the peninsula of Apcheron, the United States ought to produce, not merely two or three times, but five hundred times, more than Russia. This important fact proves that the richness of the supply of Bakou amply compensates for what it wants in extent of area. In fact, we have seen that the wells of Bakou give, daily, about three times as much as those of the United States. Besides that, the enormous height to which the jets of petroleum at Bakou are thrown upwards, constitutes a further proof in favour of the power of the mass which evicts those jets, of which the height at Bakou attains to 84 metres, as against 19 metres in the United States. In a word, the richness of Bakou is such, that Marvin has been able to state, without exaggeration, what the most favoured American miners could imagine: miners obliged to sink to great depths before finding the stores below, which in Russia are not far distant from the surface of the soil; the masses which are plunged in its bowels being reserved for the future."

The importation of petroleum into the United Kingdom—coming from everywhere except India—was 16,613,000 gallons in 1874, and 77,390,435 gallons in 1887. So there is a vast market at home.

I want specially to contrast the energetic action of Russia with the non-understandible inaction of India.

I go on to quote the report as to the ruby mines of Burma. The report says: "The Burma ruby mines, the only source of first-class rubies in the world, are not yet scientifically worked .... Rubies exist, and are worked from the layers of gravel and earth below the surface, and also from clefts in the magnesian limestone, which is the matrix of the gems .... The working is, however, at present, clumsy, unscientific, and wasteful. It is expected that when machinery and experience are brought to bear on the ruby sources, a much larger output of rubies will be secured."

Then as to diamonds: ". . . . no satisfactory results were gained by prospectors for diamonds, who visited a part of the Deccan, which is reported to have yielded diamonds several centuries ago."

One great difficulty in ruby and other mines is the avoidance of theft. While I was in Calcutta I gave £100 to a well-known merchant to buy, when occasion offered, a ruby for my dear daughter. In course of discussion this gentleman told me a story he had heard from a leading native dealer in precious stones. It illustrates my meaning: A Burmese got illicit possession of a splendid ruby at the mines; he had a hole cut in a non-dangerous part of the inside of his leg; he put the ruby inside, and waited till the wound had healed up; and he then started for Calcutta, where he cut his leg open again, and sold the ruby for £2,000.

Now, where it is as easy to steal, or buy from the stealer, as it is to secrete precious stones—plain men would say, that the strongest power of watch, of search, and of punishment, was essential. That strongest power must ever rest with the Executive Government. "Private enterprise" is nowhere in such a case. Yet the Government of India has handed over "the only source of first-class rubies in the world" to an enterprising and advertising firm of jewellers in London. Robbing them will be robbing the "poor taxpayer of India" (always quoted when uncovenanted servants are to be cheated out of sterling pensions), and robbed they will be. "Private enterprise" again! How do the Indian Government propose to account with "private enterprise" in such a case!

Now, let us look at "private enterprise" and the vital work of irrigation. I will only quote one sentence from "this same" Blue Book, p. 14:—"The irrigation works of the Cauvery, Kistna, and Godavery deltas, and of Sind, yield net returns of more than 10 per cent. on the capital outlay; and the great canals of Upper India will yield about 5 per cent. when complete. But the irrigation account is burdened with Rx. 8,812,423 capital expended on the Orissa, Kurnool, Sone, and Deccan Canals, of which the Orissa and Kurnool Canals were taken over from private companies, and none of which yield any appreciable dividend."

Let it be remembered that, excepting a few embarrassing concessions dotted over the land, the granting of such things being always, however unjustly, open to suspicion—concessions which merely stop the way, owing to the weakness of the concessionaire—all the minerals—gold, silver, iron, copper, tin, lead, precious stones, coal, petroleum, fire-clay, and so on,—are the property of the British Empire, the rulers and best friends of India. It is not as in England, where private owners possess the underground treasures of the land, and levy heavy royalties.

The vital importance of the development of the mineral resources of India may be regarded in several serious lights: (1) as the way to redress—by the production and sale of minerals on a large scale—the gold and silver Indian Government difficulty. India has to pay £14,000,000 annually in gold in England; and it loses about a third of that sum by having to realize in silver. If it could pay this £14,000,000 by the sale of its mineral and other resources, the difficulty would disappear. Again, (2) as a means of effecting thereby a large reduction of the taxation of the people, or as a means of promoting needful and profitable public works. Again, (3) as affecting enormously the employment and —the same thing in a better shape—the comfort, and quietude of the people. Again, (4) as rendering India and England less dependent on the great protectionist United States: and, (5) last of all, as giving a powerful, immediate, and healthy push along to the whole industry, commerce, and wealth of India.

Let me return once more to the petroleum question. There is hardly a town or village in India, from the Kyber Pass, and Sadija, in the extreme east of Assam, to Calcutta, Bombay, and Madras, where the American petroleum is not used and sold—superseding mustard oil, cotton-seed oil, and other native lubricants and illuminants. One sees everywhere the inevitable Yankee soldered tin can, bearing the inscription, "Warranted to contain 65 pounds net of the pure kerosene oil, from the celebrated Sun Refinery of Yankeedoodledum, U. S." The empty cans are used for water carrying, and for all conceivable purposes, all over India. Certainly it does "rile" one to know that where our monopolist cousins are driving a roaring trade—free of import duty—all over India, there are stores of petroleum far exceeding, as I believe, all that exists between the Canadian boundary and the Gulf of Mexico: and, still, not one drop of Indian petroleum has yet found its way into the great markets of the world. But, alas! this applies of many other Indian things besides petroleum.

GOVERNMENT CONTROL OF MINERAL AND OTHER DEVELOPMENT.

I ADVOCATE the establishment of a State department for the development of the great mineral resources of India. Those resources, now, are all but lying dormant and neglected.

If objection be taken to the devotion of the State Executive to the development of the State's property, or to the capacity of that Executive for so serious a duty, reference should be made to what the State and its Executive undertakes now. By the "State" I mean, of course, the Government of India in its dual condition, of the Viceroy and his Council, in India, and the Secretary of State for India and his Council, in England.

To begin with (taking the year ended 31st December, 1887), the State has made, or taken over, and is working and managing, 8,816 miles of railway; and is supervising, and will probably take over, in whole or in part, 3,902 miles of railway, which have been constructed under its guarantee. It has reserved power to take over the 595 miles of "assisted railway"; while, also, it keeps a watch, and practically controls, 753 miles of "Native State" railways. I find in the "Summary" of the "Statement" I am using, that, "on the 31st March, 1888, there were 14,338 miles of open railway in India, of which 988 miles were opened during the previous twelve months;

2,487 miles more were under construction." But no doubt the State's participation in construction, working and control, was the same as in the year ended 31st December, 1887. Therefore, it is fair to state that, substantially, the railways in India are the charges of the State. So are the telegraphs; and the Indian Government make submarine cables at their establishment beyond Kurrachee.

As respects agriculture, the "Summary" reports, "There is now an Agricultural Department, with a selected officer for its director, in every large province of India. One of the chief objects to which this officer gives attention is, the maintenance and improvement of the village field map and record of rights, which ought to be corrected and re-written yearly for every village in the Empire." Then there is a "Forest Department," "manned by European officers," specially trained, which conserves, cuts down, and sells timber, plants new forests, and establishes "fire protection." But the great "Land Revenue" Department manages the whole State property with its millions of tenants, and which yields a revenue "proper" of £22,500,000, in silver, thus: "permanently settled estates, £4,311,000; temporary settled estates, held by proprietary brotherhoods or large proprietors, £10,399,000; held by petty proprietors on what is called Ryotwaree tenure, £7,790,000," or in total £22,500,000, in silver. Then, further, a department of the State Executive manages, under the title of "Wards' Estates," the estates of minors and incapable persons and encumbered estates, of which, in 1886-7, there were 999, with a revenue of £1,849,000, in silver (Rx.). Coming to great sources of revenue, the State plants, buys, manufactures, packs, sells, and generally manages the great opium revenue. This revenue in 1886 was £8,942,976 gross, and £6,214,000 net, in silver (Rx.). The State, again, manufactures 48 per cent., and mines 22 per cent., of all the salt consumed in India, only 30 per cent. coming in, on duty, from abroad. The gross salt revenue was £6,657,644, in silver, in 1886-7.

Beside all this, the State is sole postman, sole telegraph constructor, worker, and manager; carries out and manages the great irrigation works, and all civil and military works. It charges itself with the botanical and other gardens, exchanging, through its able officers, such as Dr. King, of Calcutta, and others, seeds and plants with all the world. Under the State, chinchona and other valuable drugs are grown upon "3,052 acres of Government plantation in Sikkim and the Nilgiri hills, and 11,417 acres of private plantations. The yield of the Sikkim plantation was 225,631 lbs. of dry bark, worked up into 6,790 lbs. of febrifuge or quinine, of which 5,885 were consumed by Government hospitals and dispensaries, or by the public; the Nilgiri harvest, of 124,333 lbs. dry bark, was mostly sold in open market. The yield of private plantations is returned at 626,146 lbs." The report concludes :—"The Sikkim plantations more than covered their expenses by the yield of febrifuge and quinine; and the benefit to the people of India from the cheapness of the drug was great." Then we find State farms, State exhibitions of agricultural implements, State officers engaged on silkworm enquiries, State stallions and brood mares—both horse and donkey, and State bulls.

I think the above recital shows that the State in India is capable of developing the great, untouched, mineral resources belonging to the State; and that it either possesses, or knows where to get, the men of experience and energy needful in order to make its underground and overground mineral riches valuable, in increasing volume to India and to the world.

A great executive department, created for such a great purpose, should not only contain men personally experienced in mines and minerals, but railway men, conversant with the duties of the carrier, and men of the merchant class. Let me express the belief that such a department, organized on the fitness of its proposed members, chosen without favouritism or patronage, would, within a very few years of exploration, experiment, and organization, send to market, in India and abroad, "every year," twenty millions' worth of wealth, now lying useless below and upon the surface of India.

I may be told that this is all a dream. Time will show. If it could be realized, who would not approve? Is it not, at least, worth the thoughtful consideration of our Indian statesmen?

THE "NATIONAL CONGRESS."

WHILE at Allahabad, last December, I had the curiosity to go, with a resident friend, to see the building in which the Baboos, who thus entitle their annual assembly, intended to meet this year. It was large and oblong, the walls of well-moulded mud, made ornamental by round pillars and simple capitals in some places, both inside and out. The size was 120 feet by 80: a good-sized room, which would seat 2,000 people. The roof, of rough bamboos, had been put on, but was waiting for the matting and canvas, which would cover its nakedness. My friend and I found a number of the organizers on the ground; and they, rather volubly, explained their arrangements about the building. The contract price of the building was 3,000 rupees, or £200 in gold. The building was to be removed as soon as the proceedings had concluded. The leading personage present, of the committee, was a rich Baboo, one of a family of money lenders and owners of property, to whom a good deal of that quarter of the town belonged. He was also the owner of my friend's house—for which he charged a big rent; but was always, I heard, greatly exercised in his mind when any little repairs were needed and demanded. The cost of a broken window hurt his feelings; but any heavy work was torture in the extreme.

This gentleman, in brown turban and plain dress, a

small, thin, grey moustache on his upper lip, carried a British sovereign, with the Queen's effigy upon it, suspended by a thin gold chain from his neck. This was to show his loyalty, I suppose. Perhaps, also, his gratitude for being allowed to live in peace and usury, oppressing the poor by excessive exaction of interests and prices,—without having his throat cut. All which was, no doubt, also, quite consistent with his present attitude as a stirrer-up of sedition, and abuse of English officials in general, and now and then of English women in particular. He was very proud of a meeting with Lord Dufferin last year, after the Congress at Madras. He said, he and six others met the Viceroy, who said they might each ask a question, and he would answer. It came to the turn of this gentleman last; and his account was, that he asked the Viceroy "if the income tax would be taken off?" and the Viceroy replied, "I don't think it will; but I don't think it will be increased." Whether this rich, sleek, and sly old Bunia paid as little income tax as he could help, may be probable. A noteworthy fact appears in the "Statement" of the progress of India, under the head of "Income Tax," as follows: (p. 83): "About 30 per cent. of the amount (of income tax) collected was charged on salaries and pensions (three-fourths of those paying in this schedule being Government servants). There were 774 companies, paying an average of 964 rupees, whose contributions were less than 6 per cent. of the total proceeds; from interest on securities, rather more than 5 per cent. was derived; and the remaining 59 per cent. was obtained from other sources of income; *one-third of those assessed in this schedule being money-lenders, paying about* 24 *rupees each on the average;* and nine-tenths of the whole number being assessed on incomes of 2,000 rupees or less." I wonder if my anti-income-tax friend, of the Congress Hall, is one of those who, "being money lenders," pay "about 24 rupees each on the average." I ask Mr. "Bonargee of the 'Arcadia,'" to answer the question.

On board the "Arcadia," in which, noble, ship of the Peninsular and Oriental Company I left the Thames on the 20th October, was a Hindu gentleman named Bonargee, a very pleasant, intelligent, man. The names of Bengalee Brahmans generally end in "gee" or "gi"; and there is another Bonargee in Calcutta (Surendronath), a leading congress-wallah, now editor of a paper, established to abuse English rule and rulers, who was educated at an English university, and was at one time in an important and lucrative office under the Indian Government. Why he was parted, or parted, from that office, I know not. But he has the repute of being an earnest and laborious agitator.

While both Bonargees are, or were, Government employés—Bonargee of the "Arcadia" being a Government counsel, holding, even now, an important office, and Bonargee of Calcutta, having still, I hear, an allowance or pension from Government—they, nevertheless, deem it proper and consistent to join in the Congress howl. A Mr. Hume, who predicted (according to the admirable speech of the late Viceroy, Lord Dufferin, at the St. Andrew's Dinner at Calcutta) mutiny and rebellion, if his notions were not soon realized, and I believe other leading wallahs, are pensioners of the State. All round it is a queer position. Clearly discipline is not maintained; and it is time to call attention to these men and their doings.

Now, on board the "Arcadia" there was an esteemed merchant of London, Manchester, and Calcutta—Mr. Yule. He is a thoughtful and very able man. He can play two games at chess at once, and usually beats his two opponents. At Calcutta I learned, with surprise, that Mr. Yule had agreed to preside at the Allahabad Congress; but I think, now, I may guess the reason—in one word, Bonargee of the "Arcadia:" Bonargee was the tempter; Yule bit the apple, and was lost. But in justice to Mr. Yule, I must say that his views, as explained, by him, to me—before he went to preside at the mud temple at Allahabad, by-the-bye—are moderate; but I fear they merely serve as the purpose of the sugar with which our doctors hide the interior nastiness of their pills. I think Mr. Yule has been simply made use of. How could such an astute Scotchman have been thus taken in? Mr. Yule says that he merely asks that, whereas the Viceroy's Council is now a nominated, it should become, as regards half its members, an elected body. But the qualification of the candidates, and the suffrage of the electors, he leaves to the State Government; and I think he wishes, also, to leave a veto, always, in the power of the Viceroy. At present, the Viceroy and his advisers give to the commercial interests of India, and to the natives of India, distinct representation; and I have not heard any complaint of the selection, for instance, of Mr. Steel, of Calcutta, or of the native gentlemen picked out from a great body of, no doubt eligible, candidates. Though Mr. Yule's plan would, practically, substitute for a careful selection of the best of the eligible men, the heat and fury of an election contest, would that be a gain to thoughtful and enlightened government? In fine, would better men be chosen? It must be remembered that we are dealing with a Government whose great function is that of being standing arbitrator between hostile, and hating, races, creeds, and customs. We do not choose high arbitrators by popular election. But, would Mr. Yule's proposal satisfy the Bonargees? I will put that question in the light of facts, and I will appeal to more experienced opinions than my own.

First of all, the Congress is, to all intents and purposes, a convention: as close an imitation of a distinct representative body as the artful and clever agitators can make it. Its members are chosen under the cloak, more or less a disguise, of popular election in open meeting. Its aspirations are the substitution of a Hindu majority government for the government of the Viceroy and his Council: while, for the purpose of the moment, great loyalty to the Queen is loudly shouted out—the tongues of many of these patriotic Baboos being in their cheeks all the while.

Far be it from me to say that there are not gentlemen learned and honest amongst those who have attended the Congresses already held. But no one of those learned and honest men will contradict me when I say there is no pretence for calling these meetings "National." It is a false pretence. These gentlemen will not contradict me when I say that the whole action is in opposition to British rule—political action. But that not one attempt has been made to improve the social condition of the people of India. What about the miserable Hindu widow? What about the profane and grovelling superstitions, endowed as they are with immense properties—as Juggernaut, for instance—swarming with priests and degrading sacrifices? Where is the rebuke of the "gombeen" men of India, who fatten upon the ruin of the poorest of the poor? Where is the censure of the zemindar, who, as middleman, too often grinds the faces of the cultivators? Where do we find any denunciation of the exactions, the tyranny, the torture, the licentiousness of Native Rule? No The whole is an attack upon the best Government India ever had.

There are men at the bottom of it all who seek to parody David, and create a Cave of Adullam:

"And everyone that was in distress, and everyone that was in debt, and everyone that was discontented, gathered themselves unto him: and he became a captain over them."

I lay it down as undeniable, that a majority Government in India would of absolute consequence be a despotism; and I say that the Hindus have done nothing for their own social regeneration: while we English have done all the little that could be done to raise them up.

My attention was called, by a Mahommedan gentleman of great learning and influence—who, I should state, is, as a representative of his religion and his class, strongly opposed to these Congresses (which are no more "National" than were the "Three tailors of Tooley-street"), as the beginning of mischief, and as, especially, tending to revive buried antagonisms of religion and of race—to a series of strictures on the Congress by Professor Beck, a learned Englishman, now President of the College at Allighur. The gentleman I allude to assured me that Professor Beck's views represented the general convictions of the great Mahommedan bodies in India.

In a paper entitled "In what will it End," Professor Beck says:—"As it is my belief that the agitation, of which the National Congress is the visible head, will, if unchecked, sooner or later end in a mutiny, with its accompanying horrors and massacres, followed by a terrible retaliation on the part of the British Government, bringing absolute ruin for the Mussulman, the Rajputs, and other brave races, and resulting in the retardation of all progress, I wish to place before my countrymen the reasons which have led me to form this opinion, and to invite a refutation of the arguments adduced. We had a sharp lesson in 1857 about the inadvisability of not studying the under-currents of thought in India, and I fear that if we let the Bengali press and the Congress agitation go on for another ten or twenty years, we shall have as disagreeable an awakening as we had then."

To show the real objects of the agitators, the Professor quotes from one of their publications, "The Tamil Catechism," for instance, sent out—at somebody's cost—to millions of ignorant people.

"*Q.* Then you think the Congress will really be of great use?—*A.* Yes, most certainly: for one of the best means of promoting the welfare of India is the establishment of a Grand Council, on the lines of the English Parliament; and if persevered in wisely, and guided and supported by the whole country, the Congress will gradually, when India is fit for this, be converted into an Indian Parliament, which will take the place of the sham Councils of the present day."

And he quotes the speech of Surendronath Bonargee, to show what use would be made of the Councils which are to supersede the "sham Councils of the present day":—

"It is impossible to think of a domestic grievance, or a matter of domestic complaint, which will not be remedied if the constitution of the Councils were changed and remodelled according to our programme. Talk of the separation of judicial from executive functions, why the reform would be effected at once, if we had the making of our own laws! Talk of the wider employment of our countrymen in the public service, why the Queen's Proclamation would be vindicated to the letter, if we had some control over the management of our domestic concerns! You fret and fume under the rigour of an income tax, which touches even the means of subsistence [money lenders paying 24 rupees apiece !], why the incidence of the tax would be altered, the minimum raised, if we had anything to do with the imposition of the tax, or if we were permitted to modify it!"

And to show the extent of the demands, hidden behind "loyalty to the Queen," but peeping out now and then, Mr. Beck quotes a speech of a Mr. Eardly Norton—whether, also, a Government employé or pensioner, is not stated*—thus :—

"The day will come when an infinitely larger and truer freedom will be yours, when the great question of taxation will be within your grasp; when you will, in truth, realize that you have got something more than mere potential power; when you shall place you hand upon the purse-strings of the country and the Government. (Loud and continued applause.) Money is power, whether it be in the hands of an individual or of a government. He who has the dispensing of money is he who has control of all ultimate authority. (Cheers.) Once you control the finance, you will taste the true meaning of power and freedom." (Cheers.)

When we read "we" and "you," let us ask, who are the "we" and "you" of the present?—A band of Bengal lawyers and editors, aided by the flies they have lured into their web. The "we" and "you" of the intended future are the great Hindu majority of population—for there can be no popular rule save that of the majority; and here the majority is formed of the most ignorant and helpless of the whole people—a majority steeped in the grossest and most degrading superstitions;

---

* NOTE.—I learn that this Mr. Norton is a Madras barrister. He used to get so much per month from Government as coroner for Madras. The office was abolished in 1888.

men who believe in Juggernaut and the Suttee still, and whose priests would restore both to-morrow if they had the power: men who at this day preserve the cruel, the horrible, Hindu widow system as one of the sacred articles of their religion: a system so revolting that all humanity should cry out against it.

But I wish to allow Professor Beck—whose eminent father is known in all scientific circles, and who himself has had a distinguished university career—to speak for himself. I shall, therefore, quote a few extracts from his various "Indian Papers," and ask my friends thoughtfully to read them.

In answer to a book by a Mr. Cotton, who is now one of the Secretaries of the Government of Bengal—a Government whose returns are wanting in the Statistical Abstract—the Professor says:—

"The first obvious mistake in the book is a very common one—an exaggerated importance attached to Calcutta—a belief that Calcutta sways the rest of India, and hence a flattering assumption that by studying Calcutta we may read the minds of the people of other parts of India. Mr. Cotton writes:—'The public opinion is moulded in the Metropolis, and takes its tone almost entirely from the educated community which centres in the chief towns. No one can pretend to possess any knowledge of native feeling who does not keep his finger on the pulse of public opinion in the Presidency Towns. The people of India cannot but act and think as that section of the community which monopolises the knowledge of politics and administration, may instruct them. The educated classes are the voice and brain of the country. The Bengali Babu now rules public opinion from Peshawar to Chittagong.' It may be concluded from these remarks that Mr. Cotton is not well acquainted with Upper India or with the Mahomedan community of any part of the continent. To begin with, it is a very erroneous assumption to suppose that the only educated people in India are the people who have learnt English. This is certainly most untrue of the Mahomedan community, for learning has been the heritage of Islam for ages; and although Mahomedan civilization has fallen much into decay, there are still to be found in India thousands of men well versed in the literature of Persia and Arabia, who would be recognised in any society as educated and cultivated men. It is a mistake to suppose that these men have no knowledge of politics and administration, that they never think about these subjects, and that they exert no influence on their countrymen. On the contrary, in logical thought and sound sense, their opinions often contrast very favourably with the utterances of those who are the apostles of the new school. Being the descendants of men who have governed a mighty empire, they have very distinct traditions as to the best principles of government, and the best means of captivating the affections of an Oriental people; and they criticise English measures from a very different point of view from that of Young Bengal. They have been largely utilised by the British Government in the administration of Upper India, and many of them hold important positions in the Native States. Their political thought resembles the old Tory school of England far more than the Radical, and they are by no means so enthusiastic for democratic measures as is commonly supposed by Englishmen. For example, most of them dislike the freedom of the Press, and think that it is calculated to fan the numerous race animosities of which India is a hot bed. On the other hand, they have their own grievances which find inadequate public utterance. Their first demand is for sympathy from their rulers, and that they should not be looked upon as an inferior race. They would prefer the Army to the Civil Service, and they feel it as a stain on the national honour that none of them are allowed high rank in that, to them the most honourable, profession. But in thought and feeling they are eminently conservative. And they are the real leaders of their communities, and command their hearts and their swords.

"In estimating the political situation in India, it should be remembered that questions of Indian politics affect more nearly the fundamental basis of society than questions of English politics; and the first essential for a sound appreciation of them is to keep clearly before the mind the great physical forces which lie quiescent under the calm surface of Indian life, and which are the most important, and in the event of a disturbance, would be the only important factors to be reckoned with. Now the control of these latent forces is not, as far at least as the Bengal Presidency is concerned, vested in Calcutta. If the English left the country, the Mahomedans, Sikhs, Rajputs, and Jats would choose as their leaders men whose existence Mr. Cotton ignores in his book, and these people might begin to make things very unpleasant for the disciples of the new school of thought. To overlook this is to overlook one of the most essential facts of the political situation in India; in *New India* we may say, if by 'New India' we mean not the visionary India of the future, but the actual India of to-day, the India we see about us with our eyes—sweet and beautiful, full of attractive sights and of quaint old customs, and the home at once of two great Oriental civilizations, Islam and Hinduism inextricably mixed. But the term 'New India' has an ambiguity which, unless noticed, is fruitful of error. For it may mean those political and social forces which owe their existence to English influence, and which at present form so small a proportion of the whole; or it may mean the India of to-day: and it is very easy by starting an argument in which the first premise presupposes the former meaning, and the conclusion the latter, to arrive at very fallacious, though often neat and pleasing, results.

"The next subject I would deal with is the thesis of Chapter I., that a common Indian nationality is showing itself all over India. English education, as the author points out, tends to bring the different peoples of India nearer together by giving them a common language and a common culture. That this is a cause which ought in time to produce some assimilation of the different peoples of India, few will deny. But when he says that an actual spirit of common nationality is fast growing up, he is, it seems to me, going far ahead of the facts, and will certainly give English readers a wrong impression. The facts adduced to shew the existence of this sentiment are the common feeling among the peoples of India on the Ilbert Bill, raised by Anglo-Indian opposition, the ovation given to Lord Ripon, the protestations of loyalty at the time of the Russian crisis, and last of all, the mourning stated to have been general on the death of Keshub Chunder Sen. With regard to the last fact, he makes the following remarkable assertion :—'The natives of all parts of India, whatever their religion may have been, united with one voice in the expression of sorrow at his loss, and pride in him as a member of one common nation.' So far was this from being the case that many well cultivated and very influential men of Upper India do not even know his name. What ignorance! People may exclaim to whom the name of the leader of the Brahmo Somaj is familiar. But the ignorance is no greater probably than that of the learned Brahmo's countrymen of, let us say, Shah Abdul Aziz, the 'Sun of India.' These facts must strike one with surprise until one realises that not less than the physical difference between the burning plains of Mecća and the snowy heights of the Himalaya is the difference in thought and feeling between the Mahomedan and Hindu worlds."

Then, in dealing with the idea of a common Indian nationality, composed of all races, religions, and customs, the Professor says :—

"In connection with this idea of a common Indian nationality, some interesting questions arise. In the first place, is it desirable? This is very often assumed, but it requires some proof, for nobody wants to make Europe one nation. Then suppose it be desirable, and highly desirable, so that it is an object worth working for, what are the necessary conditions of accomplishing it? It is quite clear that if there is to be a real approximation, every community in India must be prepared to sacrifice some cherished customs. Are people prepared to make the necessary sacrifices? We believe not one man in ten thousand is, and among the ten thousand must be reckoned Mr. Cotton. For what is a nation? The word nation implies that the people who compose it have some marked points of resemblance which differentiate them from other people. In a nation like England we find a body of men united by race, country, government, religion, language, manners and customs, and culture. In Europe it is considered essential that the people to be of one nation should be of one race, but in India we are obliged to make an exception to this in the case of the Mahomedans, who, if not a nation in the strictest sense of the term, are united by a feeling very like national feeling, and derived from the religious and social bond. Therefore to produce a nation in India of the European type, it would be necessary that for some generations there should be free intermarriage between all communities, a proposal which in the East would stagger the boldest man;

while a nation of the Mahomedan type would require community of religion, manners and customs, and culture. In either case the people of India must be made really to resemble one another; and, to begin with, the Hindus must give up their caste system, which is indeed a barrier to a thorough-going national feeling in their own body."

The great usury question, in combination with a plan for removing populations in India, for greater union of race and religion, brings this, pungent, paragraph :—

"I do not know in what part of the country the natural tendency alluded to is observed. In the North-West Provinces the prevailing natural tendency seems to be for the unwarlike usurers—the banias—to buy up and cheat out the noble old martial races, Hindu and Mahomedan alike, and to oust them from their lands. And this tendency, far from offering any basis for political reconstruction, is one of the least hopeful signs of the future, for the banias are about as popular as their brethren the Jews in Germany and Russia, and are absolutely without powers of self-defence. But as for the British Government, or, to speak more accurately, 'the party of foreign occupiers' assisting this movement, bodily clearing off all the Mahomedans of wealth and good family, and importing Hindu grandees to occupy their estates and step into their social position, the suggestion is worthy of Mahomed Tughlak.* And when Mahomedan nobility have been replanted, how can we prevent the banias from buying them up again? Like that of the land, the settlement cannot be a permanent one, but a fresh sorting out will frequently be required as after a communists' redistribution of money. Mr. Cotton's great complaint of the 'foreign occupiers' is that they have interfered too much; that they have played too paternal a part; that their railways have been too great a shock for the instincts of a conservative people; but all that they have done would be child's play compared with what he now calls on them to do. The aristocrats are to be driven from the associations of home

---

* A Mahomedan Emperor who marched off the whole city of Delhi by force to the Deccan, and thereby caused infinite suffering and misery. His other acts were equally interesting and mad.

and from the lands their ancestors have held for centuries. And who are the aristocrats? By no means only the rich classes; for many a poor man has a far higher social position than his rich neighbours. But if the charge can be brought home to any man that he is a genuine aristocrat, he must be hunted out like a French prince and transported. Mr. Cotton is a humane man, and would no doubt not like to see this done; but it is the logical outcome of his solitary proposal for dealing with the most obvious and greatest difficulty that besets his scheme. Like many other Indian reformers, he does not think out carefully enough the results of his proposed reforms. Although he shows in one part of his book that he has observed some of the salient facts of Indian politics, yet when he evolves his plans of reform he practically ignores them."

And he concludes the reply to Mr. Cotton in these words:—

"And inasmuch as the discontent has a social origin, it is perfectly clear that if a healthy state of things is to be produced, it must be through the medium of the English who come in contact with the people, *i.e.*, Anglo-Indians, and not by trying to ride roughshod over them by means of the English in England. The great result to be attained is that Englishmen, Hindus, and Mahomedans, may all alike feel they are component parts, and have a share in the glory of a magnificent and enlightened Empire. This mysterious union of East and West should be beneficial not to the former only. In estimating the value of India to England, most people dwell only on the material side. They point to the amount of British trade with India. But India might have a much higher value for the English if we knew as a nation how to appreciate her—a moral and intellectual value. It is the narrowest opinion of Western prejudice to suppose that all beautiful ideals, all noble and profound thoughts on life, all graces of civilization, have been collected in Europe alone. The East, which has given birth to every religion which dominates mankind, has yet, I believe, something to teach the West. In this age of violent industrial competition, of socialism, of communism, and of nihilism; of the decay of old faiths and the pessimistic wails of philosophers and poets, it may act as a soothing and peace-giving influence on many a mind oppressed by the fever heat of modern intellectual life to go to India, to live among its people, and to breathe in the gentle influence of ideals of life that belong to a far earlier but a simpler and fresher period of the world's existence. England need fear no impoverishment of her intellectual life by her closer union with India. It is the ardent aspiration of many Natives of India and of many Anglo-Indians that this union may become every day a closer one, and that the Asiatic and British subjects of Her Majesty may be united by growing ties of affection and respect."

Writing, specially, under the head of "The National Congress," the writer says:—

"The two 'National Congresses' hitherto held have proclaimed as the chief upshot of their proceedings a verdict in favour of the introduction of representative institutions into India, and it seems to be a foregone conclusion that the approaching meeting at Madras will endorse their opinion. In fact, in the public mind, the National Congress has become identified with this political scheme, to a criticism of which the following lines are devoted. Now to many men this task may appear superfluous. The notion of violating all historic continuity; of expecting a people saturated through the centuries of its long life with the traditions of autocratic rule to shake off at once its old feelings and habits, and transform itself into a modern democracy; of assuming that institutions which work not without friction in those nations which are most homogeneous and have been longest trained in their exercise could be adapted to a population five times as great as the largest in which they have hitherto been tried, and as varied and heterogeneous as the diverse peoples of Europe, seems to many thoughtful men, both English and Native, so preposterous as to need no refutation. Nevertheless, it would be optimistic to assume that unwise opinions have no effect in determining the course of events; nor should we trust too much to the wisdom of our rulers in England."

And again:

"There are, it seems to me, at least four insurmountable obstacles to the success of representative institutions in India:

to wit, the ignorance of the peasantry, the absence of a class from which to select capable statesmen and legislators, the inability of a parliament to control the army, and the mixture of nationalities. First let us consider the ignorance of the peasantry. The essence of parliamentary government is that it is popular government; it is a device by which the millions of common men in a country control the action of the State: the will of the people is the paramount power. They effect it by keeping a check on their representatives, and so effective is that check that the eyes of members of parliament are ever fixed on their constituencies, and the actions of English statesmen are curbed by the effect they are likely to produce on the popular mind. The virtues of popular government are:—*First*, the great stability of the constitution, due to its being backed up by more than half the people; *secondly*, that the poor classes have a means of checking the natural tendency to selfish legislation in the governors. Does any one imagine that the people of India are capable of performing this political feat? More than 90 per cent. of the population are peasants. Real representative government means government subject to the control of the peasantry. The Indian peasant is unable to protect himself from the exaction of his zemindar or the extortions of the policeman. Has he the independence or the wisdom to direct the affairs of this great Empire? The ryot is a man not without a certain culture of mind and of feeling: he has a wonderful knowledge of old ballads and of the mythology of his religion; but his ignorance of politics is abysmal. Clearly he could, through his representative, exercise no control over the supreme legislature. And if he could, would it be desirable? What would he do? Perhaps forbid cow-killing, and spend the national income on temple-building and religious celebrations. Certainly his government would be a government of ignorance and of superstition. It is, I contend, neither possible nor desirable that the peasant should govern India. And unless he exercise real control over the government, there can be no true representative government in India."

Further on:

"The government, therefore, would be neither popular as the

English, nor bureaucratic as the Indian, but would be a species of oligarchy, giving complete political supremacy to a class forming a minute percentage of the population. Now the pseudo-representative government would lack the two great virtues of popular government which are generally held to balance its defects—its stability and its impartiality—while it would not secure us the efficiency of our present method.

"*First*, as regards stability and strength, a prime requisite in an Indian government, it is to be observed that the English educated class does not at present hold in its hands the keys of the magazines of physical force in this country. They have no control over the native army, nor over those classes of war-like peasantry which form the inflammable material of the country. There are two ways in which a government may command the allegiance of the masses. The one is by appealing to them directly, as in England ; the other is by reaching them through their leaders. The former of these methods is impossible in India, on account of the ignorance of the people. There is, I suppose, no doubt that although Government may protect the ryots against the oppression of the taluqdar, yet in a time of civil war they would join his standard rather than that of the Government. They are, as they were at the time of the Mutiny, completely under the influence of their hereditary chiefs, who are Conservatives of a palæozoic type ; and in some cases, such as the wahabis, of their fanatical religious teachers. This is a fact which our political globe-trotters rarely recognize. Familiarity with modern political notions, though ultimately a great assistance, acts at first rather as an impediment in coming to a true knowledge of the East, as it leads the mind off on wrong tracks, and makes it jump by analogy to false conclusions. But our visitors think otherwise. Flattering themselves that their training in Western politics gives them a vast superiority over residents of the country in appreciating the importance of popular sentiment, estimated by them by the cheap method of reading newspapers and talking in their own language to casual men they meet, they offer the Indian statesman many prudential truisms about the danger of resisting national aspirations, which, as they cannot look below the surface, they completely misunderstand, identifying them with such sentiments as are expressed at the National Congress."

And :

"To this consideration must be attributed the anxiety felt by men who otherwise show but little sympathy towards that nation to induce the Mahomedans to take a part in this annual demonstration, and thereby increase the effect on the mind of the untutored politician. Even as it is the National Congress dazzles the travelling M. P., who at once thinks that he has the whole moral dynamite of India bottled up in a room. As I said, this is not the case. But so often is it stated to be by the Native Press and by Mr. Hume, Mr. Cotton, Mr. Lal Mohun Ghose and others, that I will give a concrete example taken from British India, which, in the spread of modern ideas, is far ahead of the Native States. The fighting men in the district of Aligarh, containing a population of about a million, are under the control of the following families:—The Sherwani Afghans, who settled here in the time of the Pathan Emperors; the Syeds of Jelali, a noble Shia family which has supplied many good officers, civil and military, to Government; the Lalkhani Pathans, converted Rajputs, one of whom was prime minister of a large Native State; the unconverted Rajputs, and the great Jat taluqdars. The chiefs of these clans, numbering, we will say, about two dozen, fine strong men, fonder of horses and guns than of newspapers and congresses, are all ignorant of English, and some of them are bitterly opposed to its teaching, which they think destructive of the faith and customs of their ancestors. Of their children a small minority are learning. Probably the next generation will send their sons to school, and in two generations, or some sixty years, the district of Aligarh may have a landed gentry speaking English, if they have not been by then eaten up by the banias. To satisfy the aspirations of these men, one of which is for a military career, nothing is done, so much is our attention taken up with the attempt to conciliate irreconcilable journalists, mistaking those that wear the lion's skin for the royal beast himself.

"The claim, therefore, of the National Congress to represent the voice of India we may dismiss as unfounded. We have shown that our pseudo-representative or mock-popular system would not possess the first merit of popular government—its stability: it remains to investigate how far it would possess its freedom from partiality. Now, the fact that the cry that one class should have absolute power begins and ends with that class, is no proof that it is less disinterested than other classes. All classes and most individuals love power, sometimes for itself, sometimes as a means of beneficence; and who appreciate it better or enjoy it more than we Anglo-Indians? My opponents may say that now India is governed by one class, what loss of impartiality if it be governed by another? To this two answers are open. Either it may be said that one of these classes is more disinterested than the other; or, the bureaucratic system in vogue may be pronounced more impartial than a representative oligarchy. The first of these answers involves a thesis as invidious as it is difficult to prove: it is better to assume that in any class self-interest is the rule and self-sacrifice the exception. But the second position is real and tangible; and I hold that if government by a class is unavoidable, the present bureaucratic system is more free from gross partiality than a representative one would be. Suppose India were governed by a parliament composed of, and elected by, the Anglo-Indian population; would it not be tenfold less impartial than the present government? Our Anglo-Indian statesmen, actuated by deep policy or by a genuine desire for the progress of the people who have been so mysteriously entrusted to the care of England, represent a policy far in advance of any that could be distilled out of Anglo-India by universal suffrage. How many native high court judges would there have been if it had depended on this vote? Or how many statutory civilians, deputy collectors and subordinate judges? Would the income-tax—that most just of taxes—have been imposed if either of the classes in question had formed the electorate? The absurd agitation over the Ilbert Bill showed how much bile could be stirred up both in English and native communities by applying popular methods to India. The first essential of the Indian Government is that, based on a true knowledge of popular sentiment and on an impartial regard of the interests of all classes, it should possess a strength that can afford to neglect alike the prejudiced suggestions of Defence Associations and the interested proposals of the Native Press. We have indications enough that the class that supports the latter is not without the human failing of partiality. Its ever reiterated cry is to open all civil appointments to competitive examination, *i.e.*, to take them all to itself. Any regard for classes less advanced is stigmatised as iniquitous.

And as to whether it is phenomenally anxious to do justice to the Government that has called it into existence, let those who read the papers judge.

"We must abandon, therefore, the hope of securing by the proposed system the impartiality of a popular government. We have now to consider its probable efficiency, and this brings us to our second difficulty: where are the members of parliament, the capable legislators and statesmen, to come from? No organisation, no institution however perfect, can be a success unless the human units composing it be each adequately equipped for the task assigned him. And for the government of an Empire, many men provided with technical knowledge of varied description, endowed with the highest practical faculties, and trained by long experience, are needed. Some people think the government of a country a task not beyond the capabilities of an average intellect. It is admitted that the engineer who has to construct a bridge, the lawyer who must master an intricate case, the doctor who heals the diseases of the body, all require a long special training; but any fool is supposed capable of constructing a State, of dealing with foreign diplomacy, and of prescribing for the diseases of the body politic. This idea is as prevalent in England as here,—perhaps more so; but luckily there is a large body of men of independent means who have been trained since youth in the art of government, and into whose hands the actual business falls: there is our aristocracy, which always produces a crop of good statesmen and able diplomatists: and there is our enormous highly-educated and affluent middle class, which is the political backbone of the nation. Has India any such resources? Her aristocracy is, from want of training, obviously incompetent for the work, and she has no middle class like ours. Her ablest men are either in government service or in the legal profession. As these two classes depend for their livelihood on their work, they cannot afford to give their lives to legislation. Only when they retire would it be possible. But parliamentary government requires men to devote to it the best years of their manhood. A house composed of illiterate ignoramuses, with a leaven of superannuated Government servants and briefless barristers, could not supply the requisite brain-power for dealing with such matters as foreign policy, the land laws, the currency questions and fiscal matters, which tax to their full the powers of the human intellect. The difficulty of selecting a very few competent men for the Legislative Councils is a sufficient illustration. In a country like India, where highly-trained ability is very scarce, the State must make the most economical use of the materials at hand. And that is done at present by attempting to select the best men when young, training them for a long period of years in administration, and from these choosing out the most distinguished for the great offices of State. Parenthetically one may remark that there can be no greater cause for anxiety as to the future than the doubt whether the present method of recruiting in England for the Civil Service is furnishing us with the best material available for the manufacture of statesmen. From the facts stated above, there is every reason to believe that the first breakdown of a representative system in India would arise from the inefficiency of the governing body, But this difficulty, while at present the most serious, will, if the British rule lasts, be the first to disappear. In two generations time it is not inconceivable that there may be an educated aristocracy, and an influential middle class grown out of the development of industry and commerce. And it will no doubt be the aim of wise statesmanship to devise some method of giving these classes, which will have the greatest stake in the country and be the best possible conservative force and guarantee of order, a part in political life without imperilling the interests of other classes, thereby satisfying their just aspirations to a greater share in the glory and prestige of the British Empire.

"When we come to consider the powers of the proposed supreme parliament, and ask what its relations are to be to the British Crown and the English Parliament—whether it is to be entrusted with the direction of foreign policy or confined in its action to domestic affairs; if the annual budget is to be placed before it; what powers, if any, it is to possess over the Army and the Civil Service—whether, in fact, it is to have any executive authority or be only a legislative machine, a fresh crop of difficulties arise, one of which, the connection between the parliament and the army, is singled out for discussion."

I conclude my extracts from this Paper by quoting its concluding, and noble, words:

"The conclusion of the whole matter is that the representative system proposed by the National Congress would not be true popular government, but government by a class; would be neither stable nor impartial; would be in the hands of incompetent men; be helpless before the army; and offer no solution of the problem how the different nations scattered throughout India are to live at peace with one another; but would fan race prejudice and provoke civil war. The idea is an importation from Europe, and has not arisen, as a natural solution of the problems before us, from a study of the facts of the country. If we are to copy anything from the West, we must compare India with the whole of Europe and not with a small homogeneous nation like England. Now, a parliament for the whole of Europe is an obvious impossibility. And the present political state of Europe, with all the nations armed to the teeth against one another, and engaged every now and then in tremendous wars which become more terrible every decade, is not the most attractive ideal to put before India. Rather let us have patience, work slowly and surely towards absorbing a larger element of the diverse native races into the administration, give time for the development of the splendid latent capacity of human intellect to which every generation in India gives abortive birth, and for the great industrial future which will raise India to such a state of material prosperity as she has never before enjoyed, and cast to the winds these ill-digested and illusory schemes, the realization of which would be the triumph of anarchy."

In a further Paper, headed, "In what will it end," there are grave sentences. I merely give three :—

"Real loyalty tries to strengthen the Government and breathes a spirit of gratitude. The other loyalty is identical in its effects with the disloyalty of a wily enemy. We judge of men by their deeds and not by their words, and we judge of their loyalty by whether their actions tend to remove the soreness from the hearts of men or to aggravate it.

"Coming now to the means adopted in this Congress agitation, the essential feature is that they do not confine their action to the educated classes, but make every effort to extend it to the ignorant. This tomfoolery about delegates necessitates it. Mass meetings are held and addressed by fiery orators; and inflammatory literature is circulated in the vernacular. Only the man who believes in the infinite gullibility of the Englishman can dare state that the masses in India can understand the question of the reform of the Legislative Councils, of which they have never even heard the name. As easily could a company of English rustics comprehend the philosophy of Kant. To understand how the Hindu is to govern India under the cloak of the British name by means of a representative system imported from England, the English with their swords standing by as the willing slaves of their rulers, is a conception sufficiently difficult to tax the intellectual resources of even a Calcutta graduate. One broad issue arises at once to the popular mind. British rule or Native rule? And when the English are abused and the grievances of the people are dwelt on, can there be any doubt on which side they will decide? To illustrate this by an example:—At a certain town a meeting was held, and as usual they secured as chairman (by what means I will not specify) a Mahomedan, so as to keep up the deceitful farce that the Mahomedans are with them. He was an uneducated nobleman, with nothing but the primitive ideas of rule in his head prevalent in the savage land from which he hails. They stood up and abused the English before him, one man calling English Assistant Collectors monkeys. What will be the effect on the mind of that wild and ignorant chief? I know of an unlettered Thakur Baron in a Native State who asks of his friends when the next mutiny is coming, being quite indifferent which side he takes, but longing for something to relieve the monotony of his dull life. I will not give his address lest the Congresswallahs should invite him to be chairman of a meeting in his country, or should send him a copy of the pamphlet to which I shall allude further on, when I shall bring more specific charges of disloyalty.

"In the first part of this discussion I pointed out that the very constitution of the National Congress was such that it was bound to foster a spirit of discontent and mutiny in the people; that a Grievance Hall, as a permanent institution, would be like a running sore bringing all kinds of aches and pains to the body politic; and that the delegate system, based as it was on popular support and popular discontent, was bound to encourage a kind of public speaking and literature, the object of which would be to picture in glowing colours the injustice of Government. And thus, however strong and however loyal the hands that controlled the movement, however much they might wish not to inflame discontent among the ignorant, it would be practically impossible to prevent the National Congress and its ramifications from becoming a deadly engine of sedition.

"What, then, will be its effect when the leaders of this Congress, the authorised official heads, publish in their authorised official volumes, and throw broadcast over the land, as an example to their followers in every district, literature of an actively incendiary nature? At the end of the report of the National Congress is printed a pamphlet which, I am told, has been largely circulated in the vernacular, in which case a certain number of potential mutineers has probably been already created by it. I shall make some extracts from this poisonous tract, but I can, in so short a space, give no adequate notion of the amount of venom hidden in it. I request all who take an interest in public affairs, and in the future of this glorious country and of its gifted peoples, to purchase a copy of the report and study the tract for themselves."

And again:

"Now what does this mean, and what will it lead to? It means—if Government allows this sort of propaganda to go on—it means the massacre of Englishmen and their wives and children. For on what material is this seditious trash thrown? Not on the educated and cultured. Not on those who owe their means of livelihood to British rule, and who would be swept away at once if it went. Not on men who are afraid of fighting. The people of these Provinces are not cowards; they love a fight as well almost as an Englishman. We had examples at Delhi and Etawah. And some classes of these people, notably the Mahomedan and the Thakur, the most spirited and pugnacious, have lost terribly by the turn in the political kaleidoscope. Religious fanaticism is not yet dead. And the poverty of the whole Mahomedan community and of the noble families is so distressing, and their backwardness in English education is so great, that only a Government which was the slave of noise or doctrinaire theories would frame measures in disregard of it. Now if they are urged to dwell on their sorrows, which are invariably laid to the British Government, instead of trying to improve themselves by trade and education, the result will be that disloyalty will take its seat in their hearts. Do you think they will stop at reform of the Legislative Councils? And do you think the Congress people who have stirred up these passions can allay them? They would be blown away as butterflies in a hurricane.

"The worst sufferers by a mutiny would be Mahomedans. As far as savagery goes both sides would have a good fling. At such a period men become fiends, and the innocent and the guilty, the strong and the defenceless, share the same fate. The English nation, on whose benevolence at home the Congress-wallahs lay such stress, would forget all about constitutions and elective councils, and cry only for vengeance. But England would not lose her national existence, while the Mahomedan would be irretrievably ruined. This is why the Mahomedan leaders wish to keep their people from the whirlpool of political agitation. My revered chief, Sir Syed Ahmed, whose humble disciple in matters political I boast myself, has pointed this out clearly. No one has even grappled with his arguments, but in place of reason a shower of mud and abuse has been hurled at him ever since. He has been called selfish, foolish, childish and a flatterer. But the fact is people in other Provinces and of other nations can in no way understand the circumstances and feelings of the people here."

And lastly:

"In the two previous discussions I laid down the proposition that popular political agitation—which has now for the first time manifested itself in India on a large scale—will, unless checked, presently throw the country into a most terrible state of anarchy, and deliver it a prey to murder and rapine. And that as regards this particular agitation of the National Congress, the methods employed are so noxious, characterised by a spirit of incendiarism so rash and so reckless (more especially in the English agitators), that it has become imperatively necessary to grapple with the evil in good earnest, and to apply radical remedies for this dangerous disease."

In conclusion, I sincerely wish that the English press would publish in full the speech of Lord Dufferin at the St. Andrew's Dinner, in Calcutta, last December; and also these admirable literary articles, which I have quoted, by Professor Beck.

HINDU WIDOWS.

MR. REID, now Transhipment Inspector on the postal route to Assam, has sent to me the following pages; and, as, I think, they disclose a terrible condition of affairs, I print them on his authority. Mr. Reid was Chief of the Detective Police Department of Calcutta for many years, and was attached to the retinue on the occasion of the visit of the Prince of Wales to India:

UNDETECTED CRIME.

BY R. REID.

Late Superintendent Calcutta Detective Department.

Ignore it as we may—for the reflection is by no means comforting or agreeable—there is, in truth, no serious crime committed in this country which can be committed with greater safety and impunity than the crime of murder. A Hindoo widow yields to the temptation of "love unlawful," the intrigue continues until the *secret* of the frail fair one becomes too prominent for concealment; then her family and friends awake to the bitter and humiliating position. They beat their heads after the Oriental fashion (Europeans would beat the head of some one else, in true British fashion—under similar circumstances), and curse the English Government for abolishing *suttee!* Yet the matter is kept a profound secret, and every possible precaution is adopted to prevent the scandal getting abroad. The offending widow is sent on a "pilgrimage," or goes into "retreat" (I must apologise to my Roman Catholic friends for using the word "retreat" in a new sense); and if she is fortunate enough to survive the course of treatment usually prescribed, by way of penance, for such transgressions, reappears, absolved of the burden of her sin. But how few survive the ordeal? For the *Dai* is but a clumsy operator, and more succumb to her treatment than survive it. But oh! how much more unfortunate still is the luckless widow whose case will not yield to the manipulations of the native midwife? and woe be to her if she belongs to a respectable orthodox Hindoo family. Then they get up a ceremony in her honour, which is called a *cold suttee;* they ply her with sweet intoxicants, and cap her last supper on earth with a cordial that covers her shame more effectually than the uncertain manipulations of the *Dai.* The widow is soon a *cold suttee,* and is hurried off to the burning ghat before the breath is out of her body. (It would be a religious crime, involving the loss of caste, for the pious Hindoo to permit even his dearest and nearest relation to die in his house.) This "*cold suttee*" means a double murder. But the most distressing part of the business is when the victim suspects foul play in the midst of these nocturnal festivities got up in her honour, and manifests a disinclination to partake of the "cup" intended to drown her shame and sorrow in everlasting forgetfulness. Turning piteously to her mother, she wails, "Mercy, mother, save me!" but is urged in reply, "Drink, daughter, drink, to save thy mother's honour and keep thy father's abru!" With regard to the crime of infanticide, pure and simple, it is too common, and the circumstances under which it is practised too well understood, to require much explanation. A high caste widow gives birth to a child. The new comer's mouth is immediately stuffed with hot kitchen ashes. Thus, "religiously disposed of," it is thrust into a basket of rubbish, and deposited by its loving grandmother in the nearest river! The immorality responsible for this phase of crime prevails to an extent few Englishmen would believe possible in a country where the social seclusion of women is the rule, and liberty the exception; and the criminals are assured a certain amount of immunity because the religion and time-honoured customs of the people virtually sanction the heinous and revolting practice. It can be no secret to any one acquainted with the inner life of the Hindoo, as to what takes place behind the *purdah!* yet how few, even of the men who pose as social reformers, have the moral courage to expose the evil! And the district officer deems it safer to blink the delicate question than to grapple with it.

As for the village policeman, he is too stupid, as a rule, to be of any use—and where he is less stupid than his brother, he makes up by that low cunning and duplicity, which make him dangerous to the community. He is open to corruption in any form, and where caste conflicts with duty, he is to be least trusted. He bullies the weak and the helpless. With the powerful and well-to-do the policeman is always complaisant. But what can the policeman do even where he is intelligent as well as honest? The lapse of a widow is no offence in the law; the magistrate receives anonymous letters; many of these he does not attend to, but when the communication appears *bonâ fide*, the magistrate forwards it on to the police authorities. But even such a case is not regarded as a pressing one, and, all things considered, I think wisely. Delays being frequent, the police are unable to prove five cases of abortion out of five hundred. I have only touched the fringe of this subject; the details would make your flesh creep and your blood run cold! There are, I admit, in this, as in every other country in the world, social evils which no government can grapple with; but here, at all events, something might be done to remedy the wrongs of the unfortunate widows of India. Legalise re-marriage, and deprive caste of the power of excommunicating the man who has the courage to unite himself to a widow, and see the result.

This far the Government might safely go, but no further. No sane statesman would attempt to plunge direct to the root of the evil, and abolish infant marriage, whatever that small but noisy section of advanced Hindoos may say to the contrary. This reform must be left in the people themselves. I may be told that Government already sanctions the re-marriage of widows. Yes; but caste opposes it. What a position for the Government of an empire! It is all very well for English officials to say that the widow and her friends ought to defy caste. They do not know the terrible effects of the *Mahajan's* curse. The widow and her husband, and very often her and his families, are shunned like poison. Thus, some forty or fifty people may suffer for the courage of two. They suffer in life and in death. No caste-man joins them in any domestic ceremony; none of them can take part in the social affairs of any caste-man.

So cruelly rigid is the discipline, that it drew tears of

anguish from the most patient Hindoo martyr, Karsandas Mulgi. He used to cry helplessly when his wife would ask him when her family would be re-admitted into caste. English men and women can have no idea of the bitterness of this social seclusion—it is worse than the bitterness of death. One result of the persecution is that few re-married couples live happily together. They are hunted out of their profession, and even out of their inheritance, if they have any. And not being sufficiently educated to take to new modes of life, husband and wife pine away in despair, accuse each other of folly, and, under a sense of injury, they sometimes take to evil courses. What a triumph for caste! That the widow-marriage movement in India is making head in spite of such crushing oppositions, is a proof of its necessity and ultimate success. If the Government would only rule that caste has no right to prevent re-marriage, and instruct the Public Prosecutor to institute proceedings against the Mahajan for putting a re-married widow out of caste, the reform would have an easy victory. It may be asked, What are the conditions which render so great an outrage on human liberty possible? The answer is ready at hand. The Hindoo marriage law is based—or presumed to be based—upon their sacred books, which have been received and acted upon by millions of people for untold centuries. The Hindoo religion inculcates that every Hindoo girl must be married. For a father to have an unmarried daughter in his house, is not only to become an outcast, and to forfeit every social position, but even worse. It is regarded as a religious crime, involving not merely degradation in this world, but eternal punishment in the next. Every Hindoo girl, therefore, must be married, to a suitable person, of course, if possible; but—suitable or unsuitable—she must be married to someone, as in the case of Lubskmebai! On this subject I will just quote a short passage from the published account of the Decennial Missionary Conference held at Calcutta in 1882-83. That noble Englishwoman, Mrs. Etherington, is speaking:—

"The last Government census brought to light the startling, the fearfully significant, fact, that there are more than twenty-one millions of widows in India. Have we seriously considered what this really means? There is, in India, a widow for about every five males of the entire population, including even the youngest male child. Am I wrong in believing that more than half of these millions are widows who never were wives in any true sense: mere children, whose boy husbands, in thousands of cases, were never known, scarcely ever seen by them? Only those of us who have free access to them and their homes—if a Hindoo widow can be said to have a home—can at all understand what child-widowhood really means. The least that it can mean is, the being deprived for ever of all that makes life—I will not say enjoyable, but even bearable. Can we wonder that she should say, as many a widow has said to me, 'Your Government took away from us the power of perishing with our husbands, and left us nothing but a life of misery. Far better for us to have shared the funeral pyre of our husbands.'

"An intelligent, well-educated, and influential Hindoo gentleman once told my husband, that at least nine-tenths of the children who are left widows go astray, and from my own experience among Hindoo women, I fear this may be no exaggeration. I have dwelt upon this evil to the exclusion of other difficulties and hindrances to our work among the women of India, in the hope that this Conference, as a large and influential body, may be held to do something to seek its removal. I presume not to say what ought to be done, but, I venture to say, that if men will not before long move in this matter, women will be constrained to do so."

OTHER UNDETECTED CRIME.

But I must leave the Hindoo widow and her woes to the social reformer, and proceed to another class of undetected crime very common in this country. A murder is committed in the neighbourhood of a line of railway. The body of the victim is carried, under cover of the night, and laid across the rails. The train in due course passes over the corpse, and the crime is converted into an accident or suicide. This ruse invariably succeeds in throwing the police off the scent of a murder; and, where it fails, it affords an excellent opportunity of shirking a troublesome inquiry. It is easy to see to which side opinion will lean where the police are lazy, or interested in keeping down the bill of serious crime in their district.

If the investigating officer is, however, enthusiastic and up to his work, he will see through the deception in an instant. But, as the number of police officers who understand their business are few and far between, I will explain, for the benefit of the majority, how to distinguish a murder from an accident or suicide.

When a dead body is run over by a train, the blood that escapes from the mutilated trunk will be scanty in quantity, and thin and watery in appearance, and will not coagulate. On the other hand, if life was in the body when run over, the blood that escapes from the wounds will not only be considerable in quantity, but will coagulate on exposure to the atmosphere, and will also appear of deeper and brighter red than the blood that escapes from a dead body after mutilation.

While on this subject, of serious crimes in connection with railways, it will not be out of place to say a word or two regarding the diabolical attempts so frequently made to upset or wreck passenger trains, and the safety and impunity with which this heinous offence can be committed. When the driver of a train observes the line in front of him obstructed, this is what he does. He applies his brake, and brings his train to a stand as speedily as possible. The guard and driver alight and examine the nature of the obstruction. This done, the road is cleared, and the train is pushed on to the next station, where the matter is reported.

In the meantime, the perpetrators, who were probably concealed in a nullah, or behind a copse, a short way from where the line was obstructed, watching the result, walk quietly away: and when the police, some hours afterwards, arrive at the spot to investigate the matter, they leave the neighbourhood as wise as when they entered it. If the guard of a train in such cases had the presence of mind to collect such men as he found available, and the moment the train is brought up send them out in various directions to search every cover in the vicinity, the offenders would most probably be found.

I will relate an instance of my own experience in this line of detection. When the K. & D. State Railway was opened for traffic, several attempts had been made to upset the train. I took up the matter myself, and travelled daily by the passenger train, accompanied by a set of smart trolly-men. As the line was unfenced, the trains ran at reduced speed, and were easily brought to a stand on observing danger ahead. I had not long to wait before an opportunity offered of testing the efficacy of my plans. One night the driver observed the trunk of a tree placed across the rails; he pulled up suddenly; I rushed from my carriage, and made for the most likely cover in the vicinity of the obstruction, my men spreading out in various other directions. As I approached a clump of bamboos, two men started up and made for the nearest village. I followed them, but they gained the *bastee* before being arrested or recognized. On reaching the village, every house was searched, but the inhabitants appeared fast asleep. I went round the sleepers, placing my hand on the breast of each, and in this way discovered the delinquents by the violent beating of their hearts. This was not, of course, sufficient evidence to obtain a conviction, but it put a stop to placing obstructions on the line. The offence was never afterwards repeated.

The following is another instance of the ease and impunity with which serious crimes may be committed. A man of the *Moochee* caste murdered his son-in-law in the course of a domestic quarrel. A short distance from their common dwelling, a tiger had killed a cow, and the murderer, taking advantage of this circumstance, carried the body of his victim, under cover of the night, to the spot and left it there. In the morning the murderer went straight to the police station and reported that his son-in-law had gone to the "kill," to secure the hide of the cow, when the tiger sprang upon him from a neighbouring thicket and mauled him to death. This story appeared so probable, considering the parties made their living dealing in hides, and the fact of a tiger having killed a cow at the place indicated, that the police unhesitatingly accepted the statement of the murderer as true.

Another instance of ingenious concealment of serious crime, and I have done with this blood-curdling subject. A deliberate murder was committed in an out-of-the-way place in the mofussil, in the presence of several eye-witnesses. Information of the crime was sent to the magistrate of the sub-division, and an inspector of police was ordered to investigate the matter. He proceeded, accompanied by some constables, to the scene of the reported murder and arrested the parties accused. They, however, denied there was any bloodshed in the neighbourhood, and told the police that the man who was reported murdered had simply cleared out to avoid being arrested for getting up a *danger* in a land dispute. The opposite party maintained they saw the missing man beat to death with *lathees* before their eyes. The evidence on both sides was so well balanced that nothing but the production of the body of the man alleged to have been murdered could establish the charge against the accused. To this task the police inspector addressed himself with commendable energy, though, unfortunately, not with equal intelligence. Every tank in the neighbourhood was drawn, and the jungles for miles round diligently searched, but without success. A piece of ground about fifty yards from the residence of the accused appeared to have been recently disturbed; this was dug up, and the police came across the carcase of a horse, which they partly uncovered, but went no further; had they done so they would have found the corpse of the murdered man: it was sewn up in the body of the horse, which had been disemboweled to receive it. The jackals in this case proved better detectives than the police, for they brought the crime to light after the guardians of life and property had given the matter up as hopeless and left the neighbourhood in despair. Now, considering the investigating officer was a native, one would scarcely believe it possible that he could have been deceived by a *ruse* of this nature. Such an unusual occurrence as a native voluntarily undertaking the trouble to bury a dead animal would at once excite suspicion in the mind of any man possessing the slightest knowledge of the country and people.

THE NATIVE PRESS AND THE CONGRESS-WALLAHS.

THE Native Press, with several honourable exceptions, supports the Congress-Wallahs: as the Congress-Wallahs support their supporters in the Native Press: as always the bad, organised, over-shout the good, unorganised.

People at home should study a little more closely the question of the sources from whence the agitation-money comes. It has been denied by one of the chief paid agents, now in London, that Russian money has found its way into the Congress pockets; but he, at the same time in a letter, very improperly sent—by way of solicitation to vote—to Members of Parliament, very naïvely declares that any Russian money, stirring, is used against the objects of the Congress. I have known cases where the special advocacy of disappointed, dishonest, and tyrannical native rulers has been entrusted to English agents in England. There was the case of the King of Oude. There have been others. More recently there was the Berar agitation, more or less to bring English public opinion to justify handing back the government of the Province of Berar to the tender mercies of a native rule, which had been distinguished by gross mismanagement,* and as gross injustice and venality. These sins compelled the Indian Government to take over the control; and the Indian Government made a thorough reform: and, as regards the Finances, changed a constant deficit into an annual surplus of some £150,000 a-year, which they handed over to the native ruler. Agitation, through English agents, succeeded in the case of Gwalior, where £7,000,000, in silver

---

* NOTE.—My attention has just been called to this instance of what may occur under Native rule:—

"REVOLTING CRUELTY IN THE DECCAN.—Nothing more terrible in the history of superstition-tragedies has happened for many years than that which the local papers report having taken place recently in the Deccan. In a small village in the Chennar taluka, in the Nizam's dominions, were several shepherds, who for some unknown, or at any rate unstated, reason were looked upon by the natives with a suspicious eye. It was held that there was something uncanny about them, and a *bachcha* falling sick after being 'looked at' by one of the unhappy Strephons, it began to be whispered that the man had dealings in witchcraft. Like most isolated villagers, the people were superstitious to a degree, and when an outbreak of cholera took place they naturally attributed the epidemic to the evil influence of the shepherds. The people murmured at them when they met, and threatened them with sticks, and eventually, when the cholera had carried off fifteen or sixteen of their number, the survivors assembled in a body, and went out to seize the evil ones. They were successful in finding only two of them, and these they brought down to the village-well, where they were solemnly tried by a *punchayat* for witchcraft. They were found guilty, of course, and sentenced to death by torture. They were first carried to an open space on the outskirts of the village, and there, in the presence of all the people who had escaped the epidemic, their teeth were drawn with pincers and their heads shaved. 'Water in which leather had been well soaked' was then given them, and they were compelled to drink liberally of it. While all this was going on, two narrow pits were being dug in the sandy soil, and, when these were ready, the miserable victims of superstition—alive, but in desperate agony—were buried in them up to their necks. Then, as a crowning horror, wood was piled round the living heads, a fire was lighted, and the skulls of the unhappy men were roasted into powder. It is a melancholy kind of satisfaction to learn that some twenty-eight or thirty of the villagers who took part in this ghastly tragedy have been sentenced to terms of imprisonment varying from seven to fourteen years, and we understand that Colonel Ludlow, the British Resident, is moving to have this punishment increased. There is, observes the *Times of India*, which gives the details, evidently a great field for missionary effort in the Nizam's territory."

rupees, was found buried for treasonable use in the future. There are other, habitual, cases where large hoards have been made, and are making. All this justifies the suspicion that there are sources of supply which demand inquiry. Parliament ought to know where the agitation-money comes from; and the Indian Government should insist on having officially audited accounts; and should enact that anyone paying or receiving any such moneys, except through such audited accounts, should be held in penal consequences. The special rancour of the British agents of the Congress-Wallahs can only be attributed to the venality coming from good pay, past disappointment, or the class of mind which makes the spy, the *procureur*, the blackmailer, and creates the sort of "patriotism" which Dr. Johnson described as "the last refuge of a scoundrel." Parliament ought to know the names, the careers, and the varied pay and pensions of each of these individual agitators.

The "Report on the administration of the Bombay Presidency for the year 1887-8," referring to the native newspapers of this Presidency, states:—

"Out of the 63 newspapers started in 1885, 1886, and 1887,—24, or over 40 per cent., were edited by men either dismissed from the Government service, or convicted of theft, breach of trust, and similar offences, or notorious for loose character, or of unknown social status, and limited education, or by school boys, religious mendicants, and the like." A Native paper, commenting on this, says, this "requires to be seriously considered by all the Native Newspapers in the Bombay Presidency"; that instead of making such a vague assertion, the Government ought to have published the names of the newspapers whose editors were convicted of the specified offences, and that the sooner the newspapers in the hands of such persons are stopped by Government the better; and earnestly calls upon the Government to publish the names of these papers, so that the respectable portion of the Press may sever all connection with them.

The *Gugerat Mitrā*, of the 20th January last, says: "These, and some of the older papers of the lower grade, have by their writings brought shame on the Native Press, which ought to establish a Newspaper Association, composed of the older and respectable members of the Press, under such rules as would serve to keep up the high position of the vernacular portion of the fourth estate." The *Hitechchhu* of Ahmedabad, of the 24th January last, echoes these, healthy, sentiments.

I have thought it desirable to make some extracts from Native newspapers, published about the time of my stay in India. They are, I hear, samples of the general style of the Congress Press. Their objects are—to describe England as selfish, despotic, and cruel: to stir up opposition to the protection of our frontier, and, especially, to the war of protection on the frontier of Thibet; and to the punishment of murderers by the Black Mountain expedition: to libel the Viceroy: and to advocate the arming of the Hindoo; and the equal authority of Native and English officering of regiments and armies.

No man can shoot a partridge in Great Britain without a licence, and anyone having a gun must pay an annual tax. The people of India are in pretty much the same condition; and, so far as I know, no one in any class of life who could show his good character, and the need for arms to defend him from robbers, wild beasts, or snakes, would have difficulty in obtaining a licence to carry arms.

THE INDIAN GOVERNMENT A DESPOTISM.

The *Hindu*:—The Anglo-Indian Government has been, on the whole, more humane and just than were the native governments that preceded it; and it is no special credit to British rulers that it has been so. For they never professed to be guided by the examples of Asiatic rulers; but have declared the European principles of Government to be their sole guide. And judged by this standard, the Anglo-Indian despotism has not shown greater justification for its perpetuation than the despotism of Louis the XIV. or Frederick the Great. It betrays the same selfishness, the same arrogance, and the same jealousy of popular advancement, which gave birth to the hideous monster of the Revolution which swept away all European despotisms. But in one essential respect the Indian despotism betrays the worst evil of its foreign character; whereas in European countries in times of great crises the Governments depended upon the loyalty and co-operation of the people, in whom they encouraged a spirit of liberty and moral elevation, in India all efforts in this direction are misrepresented and opposed in all the narrow and jealous spirit worthy of a ruling caste consisting of foreigners.

The *Cháruvártá*, of the 14th January, says that though the work of administration is being carried on with considerable vigour under the British rule, and evidences of material power meet the eye everywhere in the shape of powder and shot, and though Government is raising a large revenue, still the people of India are far from being happy. There are not wanting means which conduce to material prosperity. There is no lack of Colleges, Schools and Pathsalas, of Railways, Post Offices and Law Courts. And there is the police stationed everywhere to preserve the peace. The people, nevertheless, are not happy. Not only are the rulers indifferent in the matter of promoting popular prosperity: they do not even hesitate to throw obstacles in the way of such prosperity.

ARMING THE HINDOO, &c.

The *Sahachár*, of the 5th December, says: The necessity of opening a military school in India, of officering the native army with the descendants of the ancient Indian nobility and gentry, and of teaching the science of war to the officers of the native army, is then dwelt on. As the affectionate understanding which formerly existed between the sepoys and their English officers is now ceasing to exist, with the result that English officers cannot now inspire enthusiasm in the sepoy, and as education is infusing the sentiment of patriotism into the minds of many of the sepoys, the changes above indicated seem to be required for the maintenance of efficiency and martial ardour in the native army.

The *Kalpataru*, in its issue of the 10th February, says that India is under a foreign rule and has been reduced to poverty, not because the people have no courage or intelligence, but because there is no unity among them; that a reference to history will show that under the leadership of Shiváji the illiterate Mávlás performed great exploits and overthrew the Moghal empire simply by the force of unity, and that it is therefore necessary for the people of India to regain the unity which once existed among them, and for want of which the native rulers have lost their kingdoms and have had to wander all over the country.

Dealing with English opinion, another paper says:—They cannot or will not understand that a remarkable change has been effected by time and education among the people of this country, and they therefore oppose every necessary or seasonable reform which is proposed for the benefit of the Indians. Alarmed at the success of the Bombay Cotton Mills, whose outturn is fast driving Manchester, not only out of India, but also out of Burmah, China, and Japan, the Manchester merchants are calling for the extension of the English Factory Law to India. These selfish and self-seeking Englishmen are pursuing, with obloquy and hatred, all natives who are devoting themselves to the welfare of their country, as well as noble-hearted Englishmen like Ripon, Hume, and Caine, who favour native movements for securing political rights for the people of India. These people showed all the frenzy of hydrophobia in their attacks upon Lord Ripon, and they that, on that occasion, insisted upon their right to exercise their privileges as British-born subjects on every soil, and in every country, are now denying to Mr. Hume the right of exercising in India his British privilege of free political agitation.

The *Samaya*, of the 7th December, thanks Lord Dufferin for his order on the subject of training the soldiers of the native chiefs with a view of utilizing them for imperial purposes, and says that if this order is carried out, Government will get some 30,000 soldiers gratis.

It is, therefore, time for Government to consider whether the 30,000 men recently added to the British army in India should not be discharged. Such a reduction will set free two crores of rupees from the army expenditure, and enable Government to complete the works of public utility which have had to be stopped for want of funds. It is hoped that Lord Dufferin will advise Lord Lansdowne to this effect.

LIBELLING THE VICEROY AND THE GOVERNMENT.

The *Dacca Gazette*, of the 10th December, says that those who did not know Lord Dufferin before will be able to see him in his true character in his speech at St. Andrew's Dinner. Lord Dufferin is a clever diplomat, but he is a heartless man.

The same paper of the same date makes the following observations on Lord Dufferin's administration :—Lord Dufferin, on his arrival at Bombay, declared that he would foster the system of Local Self-Government inaugurated by his illustrious predecessor Lord Ripon. But his Lordship has done nothing in that direction. He has, on the contrary, given his assent to the obnoxious Calcutta Municipal Act, and vetoed the proposal of the Lieutenant-Governor of Bengal to extend the right of election to mofussil municipalities, and reduce the number of nominated Commissioners in these municipalities. His Lordship has not carried out a single recommendation of the Education Commission. The Finance Committee has cost Government a lot of money, but no retrenchment worthy the name has been effected. The Public Service Commission has yet done no good to the natives, and very little is expected from it. Lord Dufferin has drained the resources of the country in wasteful and unprofitable wars. He has exhausted the imperial treasury by annexing Burma and by waging the Sikkim and Black Mountain wars. He has oppressed the weak. He has, in all his acts, been guided by the principle, might is right. He might have averted unnecessary bloodshed, loss of life and waste of money, if he had shown some patience and moderation. On the occasion of the Jubilee, Lord Dufferin held out to the people of this country the hope that they would get reconstituted Legislative Councils But he has done nothing in this way.

The *Navavibhdkar Sâdhdrani*, of the 10th December, says that Lord Dufferin's speech at St. Andrew's Dinner has revealed him completely. His Lordship pronounced a benediction on the Congress when it was born, but as it grew in years and strength he began to look askance at it, like the whole official body. And he concealed up to his very last moment in this country his real feeling in regard to the Congress. His Excellency's opposition to the Congress, which aims principally at the reconstitution of the Legislative Councils on a representative basis, shows that his declaration in favour of the representative system in his Jubilee speech was an insincere declaration made with the object of deluding the people.

The *Poona Vaibhav*, in its issue of the 6th January, says :— Men like Mr. Maclean, Lord Salisbury, Lord Dufferin and the editor of the *Pioneer*, who speak in disparagement of our ambition, are said to be our enemies; but we do not take this view. Messrs. Hume, Gladstone, Bright and others of their opinion are really the persons who are doing injury to India. It is the firm determination of the people of England that the people of India shall not have a particle of administrative power, howsoever learned and qualified they may be, that they shall never be allowed to touch the sword howsoever loyal they may be, and that the British army shall never be diminished. In brief, the British rule in India is intended solely for the benefit of the people of England without any regard being paid to principles of justice or equity, and such measures as are conducive to this object are strictly to be enforced. These facts are so patent as not to be doubted by any except learned fools, and they ought to be deeply impressed on the minds of our countrymen. Public associations and the National Congress are shams and will be of no avail. Every one should remember that there is no awakening a man who pretends to be asleep, and should shape his conduct according to the determinations of the English nation. Notwithstanding this, Mr. Gladstone and men of his type create false hopes in us and mislead us. We are in vain roaming in a desert in pursuit of *mirage* instead of taking the right direction. Our exertions are therefore futile. So long as we were unacquainted with Western education and there was no public opinion amongst us, our sweet-talking rulers said, "Be educated and unanimously make a reasonable demand and the generous

English nation will accede to it." We have done all that and our rulers have now shown themselves in their true colours. They plainly say, "The people of England will not give you the smallest privilege. You had better canvass your social topics, that is to say, hold large meetings and discuss whether women should be shaved or not. Contend in this way among yourselves and sit on one another's breast, and we will applaud you and enjoy the spectacle; and when you have tired each other down we shall ourselves appropriate the subject of your contention." Lord Dufferin says, "Under British Government one class cannot predominate over another." Quite true. In the dreadful conflagration that has come from the west, high or low, small or large, rich or poor, educated or uneducated, are all reduced to ashes. How can one then predominate over another? How can there be justice when warrants are selfishly issued against persons who preach against the drinking of liquor and when authority is used for suppressing temperance leagues? What compassion can there be where useful and revered cows, whose safety was guaranteed even under the Moguls, are hewed and slaughtered? What happiness can there be where, while half-fed people are rolling and tossing through pain, becoming lank and meagre for want of salt, and shivering for want of fuel, and are being starved to death on account of the exportation of wheat and the slaughter of cattle by cruel people, voluminous reports one after another are submitted asserting the well-being and prosperity of the subjects? Who could make us happy and what was Lord Dufferin's power after all? Who would give us privileges for the mere asking? Wake up, you learned fools, even now and look around with your eyes wide open. Don't you run about in pursuit of a delusion. Put the unction of Lord Dufferin's speech into your eyes. Bear well in mind that His Lordship's opinion is the opinion of the English nation. The Proclamation of 1858 is useless. Lord Dufferin's speech is the real charter of our nation. Learn it by heart and shape your conduct in conformity with it. It is explicit enough as to how far the English people will do anything willingly for you; you need only look with your eyes open. There is much meaning stored in the sentence, "The police practise tyranny over the people, because they are impotent." This expression of opinion by Lord Dufferin is worth a lákh of rupees. He has only expounded the truth and pointed out the right path. His obligations cannot be adequately acknowledged. He has not said that the Hindus are ineligible for any particular privileges. What he has said in many places is that the English people will give them none. Why should not such a magnanimous person be hailed then? When people like Mr. Gladstone perish and the country is full of great-minded Dufferins, then only the day of our rise may be said to have approached, and hence we wish all success to Lord Dufferin.

The *Prajá Bandhu*, of the 7th December, says that though His Excellency Lord Dufferin had high literary attainments, bore a pure character, and was not a bad man, still he failed as an administrator of India. And the cause of his failure will be found in his anxiety to serve the interests of his countrymen rather than those of the people confided to his care. He made the Burmese and Sikkim wars, and strengthened the frontiers of India with the sole object of furthering the interests of his countrymen. It is true he appointed lots of Commissions on the plea of doing good to India. But as his heart was not in the matter, his Commissions came to nothing. His partiality for his own countrymen was so great that he left unpunished the acts of oppression which were committed by them on the people of India, and notably Sir Lepel Griffin's act of oppression against the Begum of Bhopal. He tried to frustrate the Congress movement by creating differences between Hindus and Mussulmans.

The *Pratod*, in its issue of the 31st December, says:—An influential newspaper published at Calcutta charges the Government of India with having secretly paid money from Government Treasury to several Anglo-Indian newspapers for writing against the Indian National Congress. How far this allegation is true is not known; but if it be well founded, we do not know what to say of this mean act of Government. Instead of taking this circuitous course, is it not better to suppress the National Congress altogether? Why should the Government make such a bugbear of a National Congress of the conquered Hindus? Who will question the Government if by one stroke they stop the whole agitation? The time is distant when people will be called to book for their just and unjust deeds, and when they will be dealt with according to their merit. Till then Government officers should spare no pains to bring about the discomfiture of the poor Natives, and if they fail in this we shall say that they are not genuine Europeans.

The *Kâthiáwâdi*, in its issue of the 12th February, writes:— India weeps! There are many to wipe off her tears, but there is not one in a thousand to sincerely support and help her. This is India's misfortune. Twenty-five *krors* of her unfortunate and destitute children weep day and night for a piece of bread, but Britons intoxicated with the pride of riches, learning, &c., pay no heed to it and turn a deaf ear to it. This is India's misfortune. India weeps and *krors* of her weak and meek children most helplessly entreat Britannia's sons for mercy, but these hard-hearted men do not show it to them. This is India's misfortune. Injustice is done to her ignorant children, the innocent are found guilty, while the guilty are let off through influence, and great distinction is observed between black and white skin. Can anything be more unfortunate for India? Injustice is done in broad daylight to India and to her dear and innocent children. European huntsmen kill several innocent Indians like dogs, and the modesty of their wives and daughters is outraged in numerous ways, but nothing is done to stop it. The British authorities are blind though they have eyes. Favouritism and influence are rampant. This is India's misfortune. Hind, how much shall we mourn for you? Our heart breaks, we are pained at heart and die without cause! Alas!

The *Navavibhákar Sâdhârani*, of the 12th November, says:— Sir Auckland says that the English Government's highest glory consists in its having taught Indians for the first time "that the end and aim of rule is the welfare of the people and not the personal aggrandisement of the Sovereign." If India had been always governed on this high principle, she would have had few sorrows. But she has been not only not governed on this principle; she has not been governed even on the principle of the personal aggrandisement of the Sovereign. Government, on the principle of the personal aggrandisement of the Sovereign, does far less injury than government on the principle of the personal aggrandisement of the whole dominant race. And it is the cardinal principle of British rule in India to secure the personal aggrandisement of the whole English nation at the expense of the Indian people. It is this principle alone that can give a meaning to the abolition of the import duties, to the monopoly of salt, to the large salaries of the English officials, to the maintenance of Cooper's Hill College, and to the reserving of all the posts in the Foreign Department for Englishmen. It is government on this principle that is gradually impoverishing India.

Referring to Lord Dufferin's speech at St. Andrew's Dinner, the *Surabhi and Pataka* observes as follows:—It is no wonder that the educated classes of this country should by their severe criticism of Lord Dufferin's administrative measures have incurred His Excellency's special displeasure. It was for this reason that, before leaving India for good, His Excellency was looking for an opportunity of revenging himself upon the educated classes. And he did find an opportunity at the last St. Andrew's Dinner. His speech at that dinner is conceived in a spirit of bitter hostility towards the educated classes and the Congress movement which the educated classes have inaugurated. Indeed, so bitter is that spirit of hostility that not all the resources of his splendid oratory could enable His Excellency to hide it. His speech consists of two parts, one of which is devoted to extolling his own administration, and the other to abusing educated Indians and the Congress movement. If His Excellency can derive any real satisfaction from a boastful enumeration by himself of his own good qualities, and from himself characterising his own administration as a faultless one, by all means let him have that cheap pleasure. But the future historian of India, it is certain, will not readily accept his own verdict, and will condemn his administration as one of a very dark description. If depriving the Burmese of their independence with the view of finding a new market for British goods, if kindling the flames of war for nothing in Tibet and sacrificing innumerable lives and large sums of money in those flames, and if making the poor Indian's mouthful of rice uneatable by robbing it of its customary pinch of salt, be acts worthy of a Governor-General of India, then it must be admitted that His Excellency has done his work exceedingly well. If, however, it be dacoity to annex other people's country, foolishness to unnecessarily sacrifice men and money, and oppression to unnecessarily increase the burdens of a people, then it will be for the future historian to say that Lord Dufferin has been guilty of very grave crimes.

The *Bangabási*, of the 17th November, says that, in his reply to the address presented to him by the Lahore Municipality, Lord Dufferin has praised himself and his administration. His Excellency has said that the people of India will derive inestimable benefits from the Public Service Commission. The writer does not know what view the Punjabis have taken of this assurance of His Excellency; but the people of Bengal are not so foolish as to be thrown into ecstacies by any assurance of this kind. It is very much to be doubted whether the recommendations of the Commission will be accepted by the Home authorities. And even if they are accepted, the Indians will certainly derive no such blessing therefrom as can make them dance in joy. The English are a people who will not grant any rights to the people of this country unless and until they are absolutely compelled to do so.

OPPOSING FRONTIER DEFENCE.

The *Dainik and Samáchár Chandriká*, of the 12th December, blames Lord Dufferin for waging war against Sikkim, and His Lordship will incur greater blame if he is found to have given his sanction to the annexation of that State. The war against Sikkim was a most unrighteous one, and has been condemned from its commencement. Government vindicated its action in the Sikkim affair by saying that its object was to rescue the people of Sikkim from Tibetan oppression. But everybody knows that its real object was to open a new market for English traders. And this strengthens the suspicion that Government will not only annex Sikkim, but also carry war into Tibet.

The *Sanjívaní*, of the 26th January, says that it is not a desire to revenge the deaths of the English officers killed by a Lushai youth, but a desire to annex the countries of the Lushais and the Cochins—independent States lying between the British territories in India and Upper Burma respectively—which is the real cause of the wars with those tribes.

The same paper says that no one has been able to show that native soldiers have ever been guilty of such disgraceful behaviour as that of which the 9th Lancers, according to the late

Sir Charles Macgregór, were guilty during the Afghan War of 1878, and which is recorded of other English regiments on the pages of Cunningham and Thornton. And yet native sepoys have to serve on small salaries under young and inexperienced English officers.

The *Bangabási*, of November 17th, says:—But the persistent instigation of the British merchants, and a love of money, which is so marked a characteristic of the English people, led Lord Dufferin to alter this decision in spite of the strong protests of the Vernacular Press. As for the plea that war with Tibet became necessary because the Tibetan troops at Lingtu were a menace and source of irritation to the peaceful inhabitants of Sikkim and Darjeeling, who that has seen the English Government looking calmly on while hundreds of thousands of its subjects are dying of starvation, will believe that the spectacle of a mere handful of men in Sikkim and Darjeeling, suffering a little annoyance, moved it so deeply as to plunge it into a costly war?

"OFFICIAL STATEMENTS" ISSUED FROM THE INDIA OFFICE.

It is unfortunate that official papers with statistics are often behind the time. It is so at home with the Board of Trade; it is so at the India Office. The paper I have much to quote affects the year 1886-7, mainly, and it was not "ordered to be printed" till the 18th August, 1888. Obviously, all statistics quoted are from returns regularly made to date. All other information comes from reports, which follow on the heel of events. Thus, why we should never be allowed to follow the current as it flows, is a mystery of government.

I remember, well, how the old quidnuncs of English railways derided my proposals for issuing accounts, in careful estimate, of expenses and net profit, fortnightly or four-weekly. Still, the plan has been found to be easy and economical, and, where I have had control, has gone on for a generation, and is going on still. The whole process is based on doing the work of the day in the day, and not next day or next week. But I think if I were Mr. J. A. Godley, Under-Secretary of State for India, I should be ashamed to send forth a statement for the year 1886-7, dated from the "India Office, September, 1888." Much later, and consecutive, information must be in an office presided over by Viscount Cross, who is a man who will always demand the last fact, to reason upon.

At all events, Parliament might have been favoured with a *résumé*, in brief, of what had happened since the year 1886-7. Just think of the "last information" as to the petroleum finds, near Sibi, being given under date "India Office, September, 1888":—

"At the end of the year, the Khatum oil-field in Beluchistan was still being investigated, and it is hoped that it may pay to burn this oil in locomotives on the Quetta Railway."

Much of the information, possessing the greatest interest, is merely to the end of 1886. In fact, for current purposes, Mr. Godley's paper, most valuable, undoubtedly, is of small use.

Here are sample entries in this "Statement" from the "India Office, September, 1888." "The latest Madras report upon land revenue affairs pertains to the year (July to June) 1885-6." "In Ajmere the rainfall of 1886 was below the average, water in some of the tanks failed, and the out-turn of the crops was deficient." "The rainfall of 1886 was full and seasonable in the Brahmaputra Valley, and was excessive in the Surma, especially in the Sylhet district, where the rice crop was the shortest known for many years, and prices ruled high for a short time."

Why should the Madras Land Report be two or three years behind?

INDIAN STATISTICS.

However, here is an epitome of some of the information which it is well to bear in mind when the question of Indian development is being considered:—

The total population of India in the "British Territory" and the "Native States" was, according to the census of 1881, 253,891,821. The estimated total population in March, 1887, was 268,137,044. The difference is accounted for by (1) that "the estimated population of Cashmere, in 1873, was 1,500,000; of Upper Burma in 1886, 3,000,000; and of the Burmese Shan States, 2,000,000;" and (2) by the fact that "the yearly increment to the population is at least one half per cent." Dealing with this increment alone, totally apart from any possible additions of territory, the population of India in 1897 will be 281,543,851 (½ per cent. per annum for 10 years=5 per cent.=to an increase of 13,406,807) (plus compound increase); and by the end of the century it will be not far short of three hundred millions of souls. So much for the alleged decrease of population.

The "distribution of population of India according to religion"—"as shown in the census of 1881" (Statistical Abstract)—was stated to be:—

Hindus	187,937,438
Mahomedans	50,121,595
Aboriginals	6,426,511
Buddhists	3,418,895
Christians	1,862,626
Sikhs	1,853,426
Jains	1,221,885
Parsees	85,397
Jews	12,009
Others	952,039
Total	253,891,821

NOTE IN THE ABSTRACT.—The total of all religions here given differs from the total population in Table No. 1, page 6, owing to the exclusion of Aden and Port Blair.

The population divides itself into—

Males	129,941,851
Females	123,949,970

and it is a remarkable and sad fact that out of these totals there are under the head "widowed" (see p. 31, Statistical Abstract)—

Males	5,678,382
Females	20,872,595

or an excess of female "widowed" persons of 15,194,213. In other words, about one-sixth of all the women of India are in the unfortunate, all but hopeless, condition of widowhood. Out of the total, 16,117,135 are Hindu widows.

There were in British India, in 1885-6, 114,303 public and private, primary, schools, mostly connected with the Indian educational system. These schools had 2,806,471 pupils, out of which only 149,922 were girls.

The area of "British territory" in 1881 was 868,314 square miles, and that of "Native States" 509,730 square miles, or a grand total of 1,378,044 square miles.

The number of "houses occupied" was in "British territory" 33,032,607, and in "Native States" 10,516,551—or a grand total of 43,549,158. The number of "towns and villages" was 544,862 and 169,903 respectively, or a total of 714,765.

The average death rate in "British India," with its population of 197,585,350, was, in 1878, at the rate of 28·40 per 1,000; in 1886 it was 25·33 per 1,000 of population. The death rate of 1886 divides itself into the following proportion of causes:—

Cholera	1·05
Small Pox	0·26
Fevers	17·57
Bowel complaints	1·34
Injuries	0·44
All other causes	4·67
Total	25·33

I may here add, that the eminent financial adviser of the Viceroy of India, Mr. Westland, who resides at Calcutta, told me that since the water supply of Calcutta has been made abundant and wholesome, cholera has entirely disappeared from the area in which that water is supplied. What cholera there remains in the outside—the "country" or "mofussil"—comes from the tank districts, the Hindus washing their clothes and their bodies in these tanks and drinking the water.

Taking the year 1886-87, the area of land "shown by the Survey Department" is 480,667,094 acres, or about an acre and three-quarters per head of population. From this total are deducted in the return (p. 53) 31,540,608 acres, under the head of "Feudatory and Tributary States"; and 85,074,875 acres under the head of "Area for which Returns are otherwise not available," leaving 364,051,611 acres as the "Net area dealt with in this return." Strange to say, that as respects "Bengal" the return has this indorsement, "Statistics not available." How is this?

Then this 364,051,611 acres, the "Net area dealt with in this return," is explained thus:—

According to the Survey of India.	According to the village Papers.
Acres. 364,051,611.	*Acres.* 123,235,273.

Then, under the head of "*Cultivated*," the Statement gives these figures:—

	Acres.
Actually cropped	130,109,249
Current fallows	22,725,391
Total	152,834,640

Under the head of "*Uncultivated*," as follows:—

	Acres.
Available for cultivation	78,460,324
Not available for cultivation	75,821,460
Total	154,281,784

Then "Forests" are given as 40,185,729 acres.

It is repeated that this is all *ex* Bengal, and I cannot make the figures check at all.

Again, excluding Bengal ("statistics not available"), the figures under the head of "Crops Cultivated" are—

	Acres.
Rice	23,114,662
Wheat	19,883,040
Other food Grains, including Pulses	71,439,218
Other food Crops	3,546,347
Sugar Cane	1,478,895
Coffee	117,367
Tea	226,412

And, as respects Raw Materials, &c.—

	Acres.
Cotton	9,852,654
Jute	13,610
Other Fibres	347,779
Oil Seeds	7,678,382
Indigo	1,034,889
Tobacco	370,502
Chinchona	9,632
Miscellaneous	2,100,792
Total area cultivated	141,214,181
Deduct area cropped more than once	11,631,425
Actual area on which crops were grown	129,582,756

The area (*ex* Bengal) "Irrigated" is given thus—

	Acres.
By Canal—Government	7,019,886
Private	928,047
Tanks	3,481,366
Wells	8,811,503
Other sources	3,022,325
Total area of crops irrigated	23,263,127

Two inferences may be drawn from these figures; the one, that irrigation is far behind the necessities of cultivation, where water is the condition of food and life in so many districts; the other, that with 78,460,324 acres "available for cultivation," but uncultivated, without including Bengal, there are ample areas for the support of an increasing population.

I repeat the regret which every one must feel, that under every item of cultivated and uncultivated areas—areas under crops and areas irrigated—the figures of Bengal are a blank page; all that is learnt being "statistics not available."

The classification of the occupations of a people is always especially worthy of note. In the return before me, out of 129,941,851 "males," 48,794,195 are returned as "persons of no stated occupation"; and out of a total of 123,949,970 "females,"

86,135,617 are similarly returned. The main heads of occupation are—

Agriculturists—	
Males	51,089,021
Females	18,863,726
Total	69,952,747
Attendants (Domestic Servants)—	
Males	2,149,629
Females	651,966
Total	2,801,595
Mercantile Men—	
Males	983,869
Females	124,409
Total	1,108,278
General Dealers—	
Males	886,148
Females	286,464
Total	1,172,612
Persons engaged about animals—	
Males	754,512
Females	235,830
Total	990,342
Labourers and others (branch of labour undefined)—	
Males	7,248,491
Females	5,244,206
Total	12,492,697

Then there are large numbers of men and women described as "workers in" books, musical instruments, prints and pictures, carving, tackle for sports and games, arms, machines and tools, carriages and harness, houses and building, cotton, flax, wool, worsted, silk, skins, feathers, earthenware, glass, "gold, silver, and precious stones" (males, 459,157; females, 13,799; total, 472,956); copper, tin and quicksilver, zinc, lead and antimony, brass and other mixed metals, and iron and steel (473,361 persons). In fact, there is a full proportion of the artizan and tradesman class.

Of other classes :—

	Males.	Females.
Authors and Literary Persons	32,177	3,464
Artists	10,347	584
Musicians	187,695	19,631
Actors	58,807	40,381

Of the actors, 47,398 males and 26,145 females, are returned as "in villages."

	Males.	Females.
Teachers	166,356	4,345

Clergymen, Ministers, Priests, Church and Temple Officers—

Males	601,164
Females	94,250

Or a total of 695,414.

	Males.	Females.
Workers in Animal Food	640,521	449,205
and		
Workers in Vegetable Food	1,445,916	1,719,513

Or a general total of 4,255,155.

Against this are the—

Workers in drinks and stimulants—

Males	708,699
Females	204,331
Total	913,030

The return of "Agricultural Stock" (p. 69) is very incomplete: Bengal ticketed "statistics not received"; Central Provinces, "not received"; Assam, "not known." But the agricultural stock, *ex* these countries, is—

Cows and Bullocks	35,394,495
Bullocks and he-Buffaloes	4,786,823
Cows and she-Buffaloes	4,971,132
Horses and Ponies	898,765
Mules and Donkeys	1,054,482
Sheep and Goats	25,299,725
Carts	1,733,061
Ploughs	9,843,927
Boats	101,088

REMARKABLE PROGRESS.

We have no reliable estimates of the wealth of India, though we can to some extent gauge it by the area under cultivation, the general industries of the country, the growth of towns, and so on. The income tax is, doubtless, a great cause of deception and concealment, as regards individual incomes; and, to some extent, no doubt, it aids the system of hoarding, and, as regards the humbler people, the conversion of any ready money into ornaments to wear, or coins to conceal. I gave a new sovereign to one of our "boys"—a most kind, genial, gentle creature. He was asked what he intended to do with it? His answer was, he should "keep it and never part with it." But is not the wealth of a country simply the difference between the consumption and production of a country? In India the great mass of people, aided by climate, habit, religious dogmas, and so on, live in health and strength on very little, and clothe on less. And the amount of their individual contributions to the total production of wealth must far exceed the European, and still more the Northern American proportions. Thus, I should imagine that the margin, which means accumulation of wealth, is, as a matter of proportion—wants of one people against wants of the others—in excess of European or Northern American accumulations. That is only conjecture; but all external statistics would go to prove this; and one hears of native Shroffs, and Bunias, and Kiahs, or by whatever name the Indian "Gombeen men"—who work in family connection—go, as the possessors of millions, and as taxing the poor and needy and ignorant, as they are taxed in Ireland, unmercifully.

Take, for instance, the external evidence of shipping, which shows something to ship and the payment for the produce and the profit of the merchandise. In 1878 the number and tonnage of sailing and steam vessels engaged in the foreign trade, "entered and cleared" at "ports of British India," was, in total, 12,537 ships, with a tonnage of 5,754,379 tons. While, in 1887, the tonnage was 7,172,193 tons—the number of ships being, however, less than in 1878, owing to larger ships superseding smaller craft.

The material and industrial progress of India between 1842 and 1857 was enormous. Taking every head of import and export, the increase in 1857 over 1842 was, on the average, 100 per cent. I do not propose to go so far back; but to compare 1887 with 1857, a period of thirty years, dating from the Mutiny. I find the following results :—

The length of railway opened was, in 1857	273 miles.
While in 1887 it was	14,383 „
The total imports of merchandize in 1857..	*Rx.* 14,200,000
In 1887	61,770,000
The total exports of merchandize in 1857..	25,340,000
The same, in 1887.....................	88,430,000

To these figures must be added the imports and exports to, from, and beyond the external land frontier. Thus dealt with, the year ending March, 1887, shows a total export of £92,904,000, and a total import, including the net import of treasure, of £71,630,000. The imports of merchandize by sea were thirteen per cent., and the exports five per cent., larger than the previous year. The exports of the year, March, 1887, included: values of:—

	£ (Rx.)
Cotton................................	13,468,000
Oil Seeds	9,198,000
Rice..................................	8,764,000
Wheat.................................	8,625,000
Jute and Jute Goods...................	6,021,000
Tea	4,727,000
Indigo	3,691,000

The Government and Joint Stock Banks of India and the Savings Banks tell the same story of accumulation of wealth over wider and wider areas of people.

The Government Banks of British India had, in 1882, 361 "native" depositors or accounts, and in 1887, 6,230 of such accounts: of "Eurasian and European" accounts, the number in 1882 was 43,194, and in 1887, 58,843.

All the "district" Savings Banks were taken over by the "Post Office" on the 1st April, 1886; and during the following year the number of deposit accounts increased from 155,009 to 219,010, and the balance at the credit of depositors nearly doubled, rising from 2¼ to 4½ millions of pounds.

Testing progress by the post office and the telegraph, the

results go all the same way. The number of letters, newspapers, &c., passing in the year 1887, was 254¾ millions. The parcel insurance and money order business was "expanding greatly." The length of telegraph line and cable was, in the year quoted, 30,034 miles; the number of messages was 2,516,826, and certainly the system of "opening telegraph offices at outlying post offices" is having the happiest results. It struck me much to see the bamboo huts of post offices in the jungle, or the forest, from which communication could be made with all the world.

But a great deficiency is want of direct, independent cable communication with England. Here again comes the thraldom and mess of "private enterprise." Why should a vast domain like India have to communicate its messages of State or business through Persia or through Turkey? The effect, where secrecy is important, is obvious. The effect, where facility is demanded by trade, is obvious. The dependent thing is dear, almost to exclusion. I sent a message of no great length from Calcutta to England and the cost was about three pounds sterling. Every consideration of State and business demands the laying down of an independent cable, the property of England and the State of India. What is the objection? In principle none; but whatever the damage to the safety or progress of the State, we are exhorted that we must never interfere with the sacred nest of jobs and bad bargains called "private enterprise." An independent State cable could be laid from Plymouth to Bombay, calling at Lisbon, and on the west coast of Africa at Senegal, Congo, and the Cape; and on the east coast at Natal, Delagoa Bay, Mozambique, and Zanzibar —a total of about 11,300 miles—for £1,200,000.

Great good would result from enabling the European residents in India, and their families, to go and return home at very cheap rates. There are seasons when the

P. & O., and other steamers, carry very few passengers. The "Rohilla," in which I came, had not on the average of the voyage more than forty or fifty of both classes of passengers, with accommodation for three or four hundred. Here, again, "private enterprise" dictates its conditions and stops the way.

We hear much about the burden of the debt of India. But there are public works to show for most of it. The permanent debt in India is £92,653,000 (Rx.); in England, £84,228,000; the Savings Bank deposits and other unfunded debt, £8,789,000, or a total of (Rx. & £) 185,670,000. This money is represented by £77,644,000 spent on profit-earning railways; by £25,290,000 on profitable, on the average, irrigation works (the only unprofitable works being the "private enterprise" things taken over); and by £73,947,000 for other purposes of essential public expenditure. What other country can show a better record of its capital outlay of borrowed money?